7 STEPS

TO FIND

YOUR

PERFECT

CAREER

7 STEPS
TO FIND
YOUR
PERFECT
CAREER

A Practical Career Guidebook
with Interviews from Very
Successful People

Dr. Margot B. Weinstein

MW LEADERSHIP CONSULTANTS, LLC

Printed in the United States of America.

Library of Congress Cataloging-in-Publication Data

ISBN-13: 978-0-9760732-0-X
ISBN-10: 0-9760732-0-X
Library of Congress Control Number: 2004097343

Published by:
MW Leadership Consultants, LLC
1040 N. Lake Shore Drive, 34C
Chicago, IL 60611

Acknowledgments

7 Steps to Find Your Perfect Career: A Practical Career Guidebook With Interviews From Very Successful People was written to help you explore and better understand the process of finding and building a very successful career path that is right for you.

I owe a particular debt and gratitude to the nine interviewees who so generously granted me their time and their stories so that others could learn from their success: Ruth Theobald, David Leeds, Jennifer Ames, Shandra Findley, Nancy Suvarnamani, Patricia Choi, Steven Good, Sharon Young, and Dr. Peter Linneman.

In addition, I am grateful to Phil Orlandi who has worked with me both as a consultant and as the 2005 president of the Chicago Chapter of American Society of Training and Development (ASTD) to help me design my graphics for this book as well as my original PowerPoint presentation that I first presented for CC-ASTD at Roosevelt University.

Special appreciation goes to Celia Rocks, Rocks-DeHart Public Relations, for proofreading the manuscript and recommending changes that really added to the book, as well as helping me with many other aspects of publishing my book. She really does rock!

I also want to thank AAA Office Services, Inc. for transcribing my tapes and always being fast and reliable.

A special thank you goes to my husband who has read and advised me throughout the process and, most importantly, has listened to me for three decades.

And last, I really appreciate the support of my children, Marla, Aaron, Mike, and Mark, for patiently allowing me to work on this book; each one has had a special place in this story: Mike, who along with his successful basketball programs for children, taught me about www.joyofthegame.com; Mark, www.MWITGroup.com, who built my computers, created my Web site, and taught me how to be in the twenty-first century with new technologies; Aaron, who allowed me to work with him on his career information in real estate; and Marla, who has shared her insight with me both as a teacher and an author.

Contents

7 Steps to Find Your Perfect Career:

A Practical Career Guidebook with Interviews from Very Successful People

by Dr. Margot B. Weinstein

Figure 1. 7 Step Process

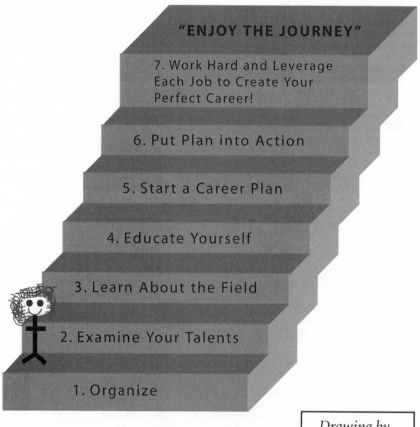

"ENJOY THE JOURNEY"

7. Work Hard and Leverage Each Job to Create Your Perfect Career!

6. Put Plan into Action

5. Start a Career Plan

4. Educate Yourself

3. Learn About the Field

2. Examine Your Talents

1. Organize

Drawing by Phil Orlandi

Introduction

Today's job market is saturated with applicants, and there is tremendous competition for good jobs. Therefore, finding a job that will lead to your dream career can be extremely challenging. This book will show you how to use the "7 Step Process" pictured in Figure 1 on the previous page to find a perfect career that matches your talents and your passions. Through information, exercises, and interviews with nine very successful people you will learn the steps to achieve your career goals. I have found from counseling adults that most people do not realize that they have unique skills and talents. Nor do they realize they have already achieved many accomplishments through volunteer activities, training programs, and valuable educational experiences. And if they are given time to examine their past and use the "7 Step Process" to move forward, they are able to develop the career of their dreams.

Since I returned to college in 1990, I have continually interviewed students, faculty members, and business leaders to find out how they selected their chosen careers. In my doctoral program, I learned to counsel adults on their careers. Furthermore, my dissertation committee wanted me to do my dissertation on leaders in real estate, and that sent me on a long journey of interviewing leaders in real estate throughout the world. In the last few years, I have interviewed over one hundred leaders of major real estate and banking institutes worldwide, such as Sam Zell of Equity Office Properties Trust and Equity Group Investments LLC, Eugene Golub of Golub & Company, and John Baird of Baird & Warner.

Here are some of the questions that have permeated my interviews:

- Why did you choose your career?
- How did you reach your career goals?
- What unique skills and abilities do you possess?
- What main obstacles/challenges have you had to overcome?
- What kind of education/training helped you?
- What advice do you have for me?

Throughout my education, I was able to move forward toward my personal goals by finding answers to these questions from people who had been there and done it. To my surprise, they were always willing to share. I believe that you can focus on the positive or on the negative. I believe in looking at a glass as if it is half-full, not half-empty. This attitude has led me to conduct interviews with people who succeeded beyond their dreams, instead of studying those who have failed. I learned that most successful people share many of the same characteristics, strategies, and goals. Most importantly, they know their strengths, weaknesses, and general career goals. The stories in this book came from my interviews with nine very successful people. The nine people in this book were chosen because every one of them believes that they have achieved:

- Financial success
- Control over their futures
- Personal satisfaction in their work—"Love their work"
- Their career goals.

Although all nine interviewees tie to my real estate and teaching background, each person has developed skills and talents in their careers that translate to the fields of business, education, training, consulting, and human resource development. Additionally, I chose people who come from diverse backgrounds, from David Leeds of Allstate and Ruth Theobald of TheoPRO Consulting, who both built successful careers without college degrees or family connections, to Nancy Suvarnamani, who moved from Thailand to get two master's degrees and build a successful business, to Steven Good, who is a lawyer and entered his father's successful business. All nine are talented and successful people, and their stories will provide you with tremendous insight into how to reach your dream career.

Finding your perfect career is like building a house. You must start from the ground up and build each step on a solid foundation toward your future. This book will provide you with the "7 Step Process" to find and go about obtaining a career that matches your talents. A wise person once said, "Although it may seem simple, it is not always easy." You must have the discipline, motivation, and know-how to proceed. I have learned that to reach your goals you must follow these seven steps everyday, even when you don't feel like it, to move forward. You probably will not know your entire career path, but if you follow this process every day, you can use it to find the path that you were set on this Earth to follow.

I have learned through changing careers three times and succeeding in school that if I follow this process diligently, I will have good results. You must allow yourself to follow the "7 Step Process" every day. You may have days that are hard, but this is the way you will move forward and reach your goals. If you follow these steps and learn from these experts, I believe you can reach your dream career. Through interviews with successful people, I have learned why Albert Einstein said:

> *"Setting an example is not the best way —*
> *It is the only way — of influencing others."*

How to Use this Book

Faced with thousands of different jobs, occupations, and avenues, you must be asking yourself by now, "HOW DO I BEGIN?" It may seem overwhelming at first, but each person has unique talents and abilities. By finding a career that matches your talent, skills, and abilities and utilizing this process, you can reach your career goals. The purpose for this book is to help you:

➢ Identify your unique talents to find your perfect career.
➢ Learn strategies and tactics for leveraging your talents to achieve success.
➢ Learn from real-life stories with nine very successful people.

➤ Select the most effective intervention techniques to reach your goals.

➤ End with ideas/plans you can use today toward reaching your dream career.

Through short lectures, exercises, and career stories from interviews with extremely successful people, you will learn how to tap into your unique talents and create an action plan to go for your dream career.

Format of this Book

Each of the first seven chapters provides:

1. A list of points to remember.

2. A brief discussion.

3. Activities to help guide you.

4. A career story from a very successful person who will illustrate each step in the process.

5. A conclusion: A short paragraph to provide my impressions of the essence of the interview and basic ideas that you should have learned from the chapter.

Chapter eight reviews the "7 Step Process" and provides an interview spotlighting leading consultant, educator, and practitioner Dr. Peter Linneman, who shares his philosophy and his insight into the skills that it takes to be successful in many different fields, and then a short summary from me of the most important tips I have learned from all nine interviewees that will help you reach your perfect career.

Throughout the book I have included appropriate proverbs and quotes from famous people that I would like for you to think about. Proverbs, metaphors, and quotes can be very inspirational, and usually hold a great deal of truth.

For each of the seven steps, this book provides you with several key strategies that you can put into action today to reach your dream career. I think you will find that this is not a typical "career book." I have attempted to put all the information into a simple, easy-to-follow format that echoes the process that I ask you to follow. Just remember the famous words by Anthony Robbins:

"There is a powerful driving force inside every human being that once unleashed can make any vision, dream, or desire a reality."

I have learned that finding and learning how to become very successful in your perfect career field requires knowledge of the "7 Step Process", motivation, determination, and most of all, faith— faith that you can succeed by following this path.

Step 1: Organize

Interview with Ruth Theobald

"ENJOY THE JOURNEY"

7. Work Hard and Leverage Each Job to Create Your Perfect Career!

6. Put Plan into Action

5. Start a Career Plan

4. Educate Yourself

3. Learn About the Field

2. Examine Your Talents

1. Organize

Drawing by Phil Orlandi

Chapter One

Step 1: Organize

"Do the work, and it will lead you down the path you need to be on; it will give you the message you need to find your perfect path."

—Ruth Theobald

Points to Remember

➤ Set a schedule to get organized.

➤ Select an activity to help you focus.

➤ Designate a place in your home/office to keep information by creating your own "Career Central."

➤ Organize your space—Containerize.

➤ Start two portfolios.

➤ Do not let fear control you.

Start today to find the career that is right for you. If you follow the "7 Step Process" in this book, it is easier than you think. Remember the famous saying by Confucius,

"A journey of a thousand miles

Begins with a single step."

The first part of the process is psychological in nature. You simply must commit the time to find your perfect career by making it a priority in your life. Needless to say, it takes more determination and preparation to set out on a journey of a thousand miles than it does on a journey of one mile, but you must have faith in this "7 Step Process." My hopes are that by beginning this first step, it will give you the energy to start to find the career that is perfect for you. Over the years that I have counseled adults on their careers, they always want to focus on first selecting a career, but I have learned that if you follow the "7 Step Process" in this book, it will lead you to the path that is right for you. Start by simply setting a time to organize your schedule so that you can focus and devote energy to finding what is right for you. Use the activity sheet below.

Activity: Weekly Planner—My Time to Organize

Day	Time	Place
Monday		
Tuesday		
Wednesday		
Thursday		
Friday		
Saturday		
Sunday		

Select an Activity to Help You Focus

Next, you should select an activity that will allow you to organize your thoughts to launch your new career; preferably you should do this for at least thirty minutes, five to six days a week. Some people need quiet time to focus their thoughts by lying in bed before going to sleep, sitting on a park bench, or writing in a journal, while others like to do it by jogging or walking. Still others may prefer a combination of writing and exercising.

I like to keep a stash of paper handy at all times so I can jot down thoughts as they come to me. Usually for me, it's either a blank pad of paper or sometimes a calendar in a day planner. I workout for forty minutes a day, six days a week, and that's when I reflect on my notes. You need to determine your activity now in order to make a firm commitment to take the time to focus your energy on your career. You may find one of the following activities will work for you:

- Journal writing
- Swimming
- Walking
- Running
- Meditating
- Yoga
- Hiking
- Note taking

- Sitting in a quiet place such as a park bench, your bed, your couch, etc.
- Walking your dog, if you have one.

Putting it in writing makes it seem more "real" and increases the likelihood that you will follow through. So I invite you to use the activity below to make it official.

Activity: I Will Commit to the Following Action Plan

What activity will I do?	When will I do it?	Where will I do it?	How much time will I devote to it?

Designate a Place to Keep Your Information

The process of creating a new career may generate lots and lots of paperwork. That's why you must have a place, preferably in your home or office, to store and organize your information. Think of this place as "Career Central." It should be large enough to contain everything. This information may be in the form of books, newspaper articles, or print-outs from Web sites, as well as all the personal information that relates to the jobs that you have held, your education, certificates, awards, etc. Getting physically organized helps you unclutter your mind and focus on what you want.

An ideal location for your Career Central might be near your computer, phone, and a fax machine. You might start by organizing your material in a bookshelf, wall unit, or filing cabinet, and then build onto it for the rest of your life. If you are like me, you will learn a lot from books. So make sure your Career Central is big enough to hold plenty of them, and big enough to expand as you gather information throughout your career life.

Organize Your Space—Containerize

If you are to do a thorough job of exploring and researching, you will need containers of some sort in which to store and compartmentalize your information. Not only is this a practical matter, but seeing things neatly divided also provides a psychological boost. You can acquire these containers after you have stacked some of the early information that you've gathered and have a rough idea of how much will be in each stack. At first, you can place everything in stacks on shelves. As you get more organized, you can either reuse containers from your home or office or buy new containers.

You can usually go online to different Web sites and look up all the different types of containers, file folders, and so forth that are available. Then, once you get an idea of what is on the market, you can go to stores and buy what you need. Clear, plastic containers with sliding drawers are very convenient because they hold a lot of information, stack on top of each other, and let you see what's inside them. Also, colored file folders can be used to organize material by subjects.

Start Two Portfolios

A portfolio should hold all your pertinent career material, such as copies of your degrees, résumé or curriculum vitae, awards, representation of your work, literature about professional organizations, etc. It is very convenient to have all your career information in a notebook or briefcase. You should set up two portfolios: one formal notebook to keep all the information in one place so that you are ready for job interviews and opportunities, and a "work in progress" notebook that you can add to as you gather new documents. At first, just place dividers inside with titles as shown on the next page.

Table of Contents for Your Portfolio

I. Degrees and Transcripts

II. Résumé or Curriculum Vitae and References

III. Autobiography (This document is optional in formal portfolio if too personal to show.)

IV. Awards and Licenses

V. Philosophy and Professional Goals

VI. List of Professional Memberships

VII. Samples of Your Work

In chapter two you will learn how to develop each section of your portfolio. For now, I just want you to have a basic setup. If you already have your résumé/curriculum vitae, degrees in education/training, or other material, you will have a place to put them now. As I acquire new awards and educational documents, I always begin by placing them in front of the correct section, and then I formalize the material at a later date. The next chapter will tell you how to go about developing your portfolio.

Do Not Let Fear Control You

As in every new challenge you undertake, you may feel some anxiety and perhaps even a little fear, but do not let it stand in your way. If you do nothing in your career, you will be at the same place (or even in a lesser one) six months from now. I believe that you should follow the words in a book by Susan Jeffers titled *"Feel the Fear and Do It Anyway."*

According to Susan Jeffers, author of *Feel the Fear and Do It Anyway*, "the five truths about fear are:
1. The fear will never go away as long as I continue to grow.
2. The only way to get rid of fear of doing something is to go out and do it.
3. The only way to feel better about myself is to go out and do it.
4. And not only am I going to experience the fear whenever I am in unfamiliar territory, but so is everyone else.
5. Pushing through fear is less frightening than living with the underlying fear that comes from the feeling of helplessness" (p. 30).

In fact, you may want to follow her steps for moving past the fear. Although you should not let fear control you, I have learned that you need to accept that it is inescapable, and in some ways desirable, and a companion for anyone launching a new endeavor. The interview next should offer you insight into how you can use fear to help you uncover your real career path to reach your peak.

Interview with Ruth L. Theobald

Ruth L. Theobald is a successful businesswoman who is making a six-figure income, a recognized trainer/teacher and consultant in real estate, a writer with her own monthly column called "Ask Dr. Ruth" in *Affordable Housing Magazine*, and an author of a recently released book, *The Wisdom of Our Burdens*. Ruth decided to organize her thoughts to move forward in her successful career and achieve a level of financial and personal success that she had only pictured in her dreams. This process led her to achieve new levels of career success, earn more money, and start writing a series of books—all while developing a healthy lifestyle. Pictured below is Ruth's caricature from her monthly column in *Affordable Housing Magazine*.

Biography

Ruth L. Theobald, CPM®, HCCP, is president of TheoPRO Compliance & Consulting, Inc. (TheoPRO), a Milwaukee-based company that produces seminars and workshops around the country on the management of tax credit housing. TheoPRO also provides a variety of services including approval, review, and audit services, and special projects. The firm's clients include investors and syndicators, developers, and management agents of tax credit housing around the country. Currently it is the only *public* provider of the Housing Credit Certified Professional (HCCP) review and exam.

Career Background

Ruth has more than twenty-three years of experience in property management in the Midwest, particularly in Wisconsin. In 1981, she began working in property management. In 1987, she joined Affiliated Capital Corporation (ACC), a full-service property management company based in Wisconsin. Soon after, she became the vice president and director of property management for ACC. In this position, Ruth provided training, marketing, management, and consulting on many forms of government-subsidized housing throughout the United States. She also became involved in the design, training, and sale of the new software technology called ACCuCERT. Ruth has more than eighteen years of day-to-day management and marketing of real estate properties experience and more than seventeen years' experience designing and conducting training seminars and consulting with companies on issues related to subsidized housing properties.

Professional Affiliations

Ruth is a licensed real estate broker and a certified property manager (CPM). She is a member of the Institute of Real Estate Management (IREM), and she was the 1996 president of the Milwaukee chapter. Since 1994, she has been a member of the IREM 101 course faculty and received its "Academy of Excellence" award for teaching in 1995. She has also been a part-time faculty member at Waukesha County Technical College. She is a training partner for the NAHB's HCCP certification course and exam. Ruth has written for the *Journal of Property Management,* and has also lectured and published in many areas in real estate across the country. Ruth has been a featured speaker at state and national conferences, including the Multi-Housing World conferences and IREM. She also has been featured in a national video, "Compliance: Managing Tax Credits," produced by the Consortium for Housing Assistance Managers in Washington.

Set Aside Time

Q: In the last few years, in addition to your other responsibilities, you started a consulting business and began writing books. How did you decide to take the time to focus on the new directions of your career?

THEOBALD: "First, I had to give myself permission to make the time, because when you own a company, you can be busy twenty-four hours a day. So I had to make the commitment to say, 'No, this is important to me,' and I needed to set the time aside to organize. Once I started giving myself the time, surprisingly, the company prospered."

Create Space for Home/Office

Q: When you began to move your career in a new direction, did you have a place in your home or your office where you put information that you wanted to work on in your career?

THEOBALD: "Yes. At first, I organized a room in my home where I would go to do my meditation and writing in the morning. The room has a computer, but I never journal on the computer. I process the information in my head during meditation or other activities. Then, I always handwrite everything, and later I go and put it on the computer."

Q: As your business prospered, did you continue to organize your business space?

THEOBALD: "Yes. Over the course of time, I have moved my office out of my home, and I have put it in a separate building. I rented myself a writing studio where I keep my information."

Select an Activity to Help You Focus

Q: What influenced you to select writing in a journal as an activity to help you analyze your situation?

THEOBALD: "I have always frequented bookstores, and since reading the book *The Artist's Way: A Spiritual Path to Higher Creativity* by Julia Cameron more than eight years ago, it has become a ritual for me to read at night before I go to sleep and write in my journal every morning. In the book, Cameron says that inside every person there is an artist and you can discover this artist in yourself by writing. Cameron calls this the morning pages. She suggests that you commit to twelve weeks of writing every morning for thirty minutes. Cameron adds that you do not have to have a structure for what you write, but you must make a commitment to write first thing when you get up every morning. Cameron's book hit me at a time when I had this sense that there was something more to my life, and this was before I started my own business. At that time, I was still doing property management for Affiliated Capital."

Q: How has writing helped you analyze your career goals?

THEOBALD: "Everyone has to do what works for them, but writing helped me focus and clarify my thoughts so that I could start to move my career forward. It has been therapy for me. It gave me what I needed to be more financially successful in my life and in my career. I had gotten to this point where I was stuck in my next career moves. Before I fell asleep one night, I realized that I was sick to death of how much money I made and how much I spent. I certainly had not managed my money well, and I knew that there was something wrong with this picture. I finally asked myself, 'What is going on with my money?' Then that night I had this dream, and afterward, I set aside thirty minutes every morning to write down my thoughts on the subject in my journal. And the first issue that I saw was money, which is a very superficial issue. And through writing, I was finally able to look at it and say, 'Why do I have an issue with money?' From that time on, I finally decided to confront this problem and start to find the answer.

The more I wrote in my journal, the more honest I got with myself: I was finally willing to look at the real issues in my life. It was the beginning of this real journey toward what my life was really all about. It has been the vehicle by which I have taken the journey to learn who I am and what I believe in so that I can reach even higher career goals. It has been absolutely life changing."

Q: What did you learn was behind your financial issues?

THEOBALD: "I was raised to believe that the role women were supposed to play was very much subservient to men. And I thought that I never bought it, but I realize now that I lived it. I was afraid not to live that life because of the consequences of not following the traditional roles. Until I got older, I did not have the courage to acknowledge what there was inside of me, because I had been taught not to. I had to get to the point where I acknowledged and gave credence to the things that were inside of me that I was passionate about. I had to say to myself, 'I don't believe that it is woman's role in society to be subservient, and it is certainly not my role in society.' I had to tell myself the truth."

Q: By continuing to write, have you been able to solve your financial and personal issues?

THEOBALD: "Yes. As I continued to take the time to write about the subject, my money problems have resolved themselves. Writing my book, *The Wisdom of Our Burdens*, under my married name of Ruth Theobald Probst, helped me take a journey from a life of being told what I was supposed to believe in religion to finding my personal truths for my career. Through writing, I got the message of the story for my first book of three volumes called *The Wisdom of Our Burdens*. It is a fable that came to me one night in a dream while I was struggling with some financial issues in my life and wondering why I could not overcome them. The next morning I started writing. The character is not me. She has her own identity and her own problems. But she goes on this journey through a medieval castle and meets some interesting characters who tell her that her real issue is not with money but with several other very incredible things. It tells her that she will find inside herself the things that she cares about, that she loves, and that bring her delight and joy."

Q: How have you been able to go from being employed to owning your own business?

THEOBALD: "Since I have taken the time to focus on my career, it has helped me use my ability to move from being employed, to being a majority partner in a new company, to being a partner, and finally, to being completely on my own. I started working in the field of property management in 1981. And in 1987, I started working for Affiliated Capital. I worked very closely with the Milwaukee developer. For fourteen years, I helped him on the development side of the business and also managed his multi-family real estate division. We had also developed a tax credit consulting business together, and I was really the nucleus of this training business. Over the years, I had grown personally and financially in every way, and I kept asking him, 'Can I please be a partner?' And he'd say, 'No. I don't want any partners.' Finally, I had built enough of a client base that I got strong enough to ask him if I became an independent consultant and could build a business, would he be my partner? And so, we partnered in 1998, and he gave me a piece of ownership in the software, and I gave him a piece of ownership in the consulting business. As I continued to focus on my career, I realized that I needed to be completely on my own. So in May of 2001, we un-partnered and I changed the company name from Affiliated Compliance and Consulting to TheoPRO Consulting. Since I have been on my own, the company has grown dramatically. In addition, I have now formed an educational company for my books and journals called Lifemark Institute for Greatness. It may work for other people to be dependent on somebody else financially, but it never worked for me. Complete ownership of my career somehow gives me a sense of being a whole person."

Work Past Your Fears

Q: Did fear almost stop you from pursuing your dreams?

THEOBALD: "Yes. I was born with a heavy dose of fear that I have confronted all my life. For many years, when I felt the fear, I stopped moving forward, and I would not let myself listen to what I thought because I was too afraid of the consequences."

Q: How did you deal with your fears?

THEOBALD: "I learned that I must walk right through my fears, because I believe that I am on the right path for me. And if something bad happens, then there is something else that is supposed to direct me down another path. I live with the fear in my business that someone might sue me, that one person could decide that they didn't like something I said or did, and their tax credit project crashed and burned, and they could hold me responsible. I live with the reality every day that I could be sued in spite of what I have done. I try to protect myself; I have insurance. At any given time, the cash coming into this company could just dry up. If I say something wrong in public, perhaps nobody would hire me anymore.

"Every day I stay on this journey to face my fears head on and not let them stop me. And once I took that first step to start walking through the fear and say to myself continually, 'I am afraid of this, but I believe in this too much so I am going to take each step and do it anyway. If that happens, I accept that as part of life, and I just set it aside because there is nothing that I can do to stop myself from thinking those fearful thoughts, but I have to move forward past that fear in order to reach my goals.' I have learned that fear in a career acts as an illusion that I must be willing to walk right through the middle of and demonstrate that I am not going to stop pursuing my passion. When I do this, the fear goes away. I have had to learn to give myself permission to place new thoughts in my mind of what is wonderful and possible in my career. I realize now how rich life can be, and how full and how utterly magnificent it can be, and that fear is a good thing. I realize now that fear really should be my friend."

Continue Taking Time to Organize

Q: Do you continue to take the time to write each day?

THEOBALD: "Absolutely. I give myself the time to write every day. Today, I am at the point where I travel a lot, but I have learned to write anywhere I am, whether it is on a plane or in a hotel room. When I am home, I give myself two hours every morning."

Q: Has continuing to write and organize your thoughts helped you to manage several different aspects of your career at the same time?

THEOBALD: "Yes. Since I have given myself permission to journal and organize my time, thoughts, and office, my tax credit business has prospered. Earlier this year I had a career crisis where I felt like I would have to let go of my tax credit business in order to do this other business. However, what has happened quite wonderfully is that my perspective has changed. I am in a blending pattern, and I have found a wonderful assistant who travels with me now. She helps me work on my books, and she helps me set up for seminars. I'm learning how to do both right now. It has all been beautifully tied together in a way that I can hardly describe. It is possible that in the future I will have to make a choice, but right now I don't see that. I love both career paths. Putting this together has gotten me into a really good place in my life. It is incredible—for both financial and personal growth.

"Before writing and taking the time to focus on my career, mostly I would change on gut instinct and serendipitous and intuitive sensitivities, but this time I really focused on my talents and goals.

For example, I wanted to self-publish my books, but I knew that I could not do all the work myself. So I went down the path of trying to find people who could help me. And I found Mark Victor Hansen's tapes on self-publishing, which took me to the self-publishing manual, which took me to Ellen Reid's book *Shepherding*. It's just like that. Being open to change and growth leads you to new relationships that, in turn, will lead you down the career path you need to be to reach what you were sent on this Earth to do."

Advice on Success from Ruth

Q: What would you say to others who want to overcome their fears and pursue their dream career?

THEOBALD: "First, I would say, you are so much more than what you fear. Inside of you there is such incredible greatness. Each person possesses such an incredible beauty, wonder, and magnificence that you can use to reach new heights in your career path. When you confront your fears, things you were afraid of, you are not afraid of anymore. But you must make the choice of not letting the fear stop you.

"My first book, *The Wisdom of Our Burdens*, is based on the principles that I have learned from my experiences. When you get socked with a burden that you think you can not overcome, there is a gift in this message or in that problem. Once you explore your fears and find out what the real message is, you can be very successful. Fear stops the journey for most people, but fear is actually a smoke screen. Most people stop in front of this shadow and it prevents them from reaching their true calling; I had done it all my life. Fear is a hint that you are moving exactly in the right direction. Fear becomes kind of a companion to tell you that this negative thing *could* happen, but you need to do it anyway.

"I have learned that a common problem for people who work in a job all their life, or many jobs, is that they never get to this point for themselves where they can focus on the possibilities. I have learned that your instincts will tell you what is right for you, but you have to make a decision on how to organize to proceed. I would ask you, 'Why stop where you are now?' You must organize your time, space and life so that you can go after your real purpose for being on this Earth and pursuing a career that is right for you. You need to learn:

- How you got where you are in your career
- What you should be doing in your career
- How to give yourself permission to pursue it.

Once you make a decision to organize, analyze your path, and take steps to reach your goals, you will be able to move past your fears into a much fuller and more successful career than you could have imagined!"

Q: In closing, would you say to others that if you take the time to sit down, reflect on your thoughts, and organize your space, it will move your career forward?

THEOBALD: "Yes, absolutely. Do the work, and it will lead you down the path you need to be on; it will give you the message you need to find your perfect path. The problems and fears will not leave. I tie it back to this problem I have had historically with money. I have been poor, and I have had money. I have found that your problem does not leave until you listen to the message it has for you and use it to move your career forward. If you do not take the time to focus on your real career purpose, you will not reach your full potential."

Author's Concluding Tip

Start the process of finding your perfect career by simply making a commitment to organize your time, your space, and your thoughts to make this a priority in your life. Remember, fear will probably always be with you, but if you use the seven steps in this book, you can and will move forward as you begin your journey.

Step 2: Examine Your Talents

Interview with David Leeds

"ENJOY THE JOURNEY"

7. Work Hard and Leverage Each Job to Create Your Perfect Career!

6. Put Plan into Action

5. Start a Career Plan

4. Educate Yourself

3. Learn About the Field

2. Examine Your Talents

1. Organize

Drawing by Phil Orlandi

Chapter Two
Step 2: Examine Your Talents

"Do a portfolio. Do an autobiography. Do a vitae or a résumé. All of those things give you a history of who you are so that you can move forward."

—David Leeds

Points to Remember

➤ Build your portfolio.

➤ Obtain certified copies of your degrees, certificates, licenses, and transcripts.

➤ Examine the factors for choosing your career.

➤ Write your autobiography.

➤ Discover yourself.

By now you have set aside some time in your schedule to examine your talents and have organized a place to store your career information. You are now ready for Step Two. In this chapter you will learn how to build your portfolio and complete some helpful activities. You will also read an insightful interview with David Leeds, a successful executive at Allstate and returning adult student at DePaul University. This chapter is designed to help you learn about your specific talents so you can reach your career goals. As in Step One, you will begin by making time to learn about yourself through activities that will enable you to get in touch with your unique talents. I firmly believe that each person has his or her own one-of-a-kind path and must follow it wherever it leads. Consider the message of Robert Frost's lovely poem:

Two roads diverged in a wood, and I –
I took the one less traveled by,
And that has made all the difference.

Build Your Portfolio

First, you need to develop two career portfolios. Don't worry. A portfolio is nothing intimidating: just a binder that contains all of your important career information. I suggest that you create two portfolios: one is a "formal" portfolio to be used to show in order to get a job, a speaking engagement, etc. The second portfolio is your "work in progress." (See sidebar for more explanation.)

As you go through the process of building two portfolios, one formal and one in progress, keep note paper handy to keep track of what you have to do next to get copies of your material in your informal portfolio that I will refer to as Portfolio #2. Although you can certainly customize your portfolio in any way that works for you, I recommend setting it up with the following sections:

Table of Contents

I. Degrees and Transcripts

II. Résumé or Curriculum Vitae and References

III. Autobiography

IV. Awards and Licenses

V. Philosophy and Professional Goals

VI. List of Professional Memberships

VII. Samples of Your Work

YOU NEVER KNOW WHAT IS GOING TO HAPPEN IN LIFE. IT IS BETTER TO BE PREPARED . . . ESPECIALLY IN TODAY'S UNCERTAIN WORK WORLD. You may use your documents only to further your writing, speaking, or other "extra" career-related activities, but it is good to have them handy.

Why I Keep a Second "Work in Progress" Portfolio

When I returned to college, I was asked to develop my portfolio, and do exercises like the ones that I am suggesting for you to complete. It was very helpful to me. I have found that by keeping a second portfolio, one I call my "Work in Progress," I can easily store new, "unfinalized" material that I want to review later to possibly use in my formal portfolio.

For example, I place works in progress, extra letters of recommendation, and personal documents such as my autobiography that I do not want to carry to many interviews.

Also, in my Portfolio #2 I store my current dues and membership documents for professional organizations. I have found that professional organizations often send me renewal notices for membership way ahead of my yearly due date. If I didn't keep accurate records, I would end up paying for a year membership ahead of due date and really only be receiving about ten months for my yearly payment.

Obtain Certified Copies of Your Degrees, Certificates, Transcripts, and Licenses

For section one of your portfolio, Degrees and Transcripts, you need to obtain certified copies of your college degrees and transcripts of courses in the program. If you don't already have them, start by calling the college or university for copies. I advise you to get at least one extra sealed set of your degrees so that if you need to go back to school, you have a certified copy. Most programs require that the degree information be provided in a sealed envelope from the college or university. Sometimes you can order this information online through a secured site with a credit card. Once you have obtained copies, you should always make a few extra unofficial copies to keep in your formal portfolio to take on interviews.

You need to get copies of all your official education and training transcripts including:

- Degrees from schools and universities
- Any continuing education courses
- Training programs completed
- Professional certificates or designations
- Any certified programs such as CPR
- State licenses.

You should always keep three official copies for yourself, one in each of your two portfolios and one extra, and several unofficial copies to give to people. For instance, keep one "sealed" copy in case you need to go back to school, one for Portfolio #1, one for

Portfolio #2, and several extras to keep in enclosed letters to give to people.

Activity: Plans to Gather Transcripts and Certificates

What certificate(s) do I need to obtain?	Where is it located?	How am I going to get it?	When will I get it?	Cost per transcript
1.				
2.				
3.				
4.				
5.				
6.				
7.				
8.				

In the second area of your portfolio, titled "Curriculum Vitae and References," you should place an updated copy of your résumé or curriculum vitae (which is a life statement for an academic job) and three letters of reference. My daughter is a schoolteacher, and she always keeps three current letters of recommendation from people and parents she works with so that she can obtain a summer position, do tutoring, or acquire bookings for seminars and speaking engagements.

Examine the Factors for Choosing Your Career

In order to develop your portfolio, you must be aware of all the factors that go into making a career decision. All the areas in Figure 2

Figure 2. Your Individual Career Pie

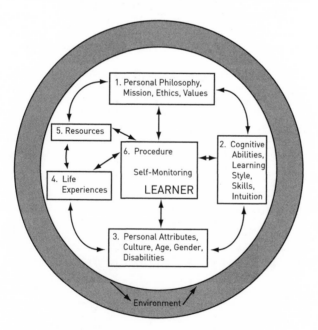

must be explored as part of your career choice. You must understand and discover how each affects the "total" that makes you "you." You must learn:

- All the factors that go into making a career choice
- How you can use past experiences to benefit your future
- How to define personal career objectives
- How to identify your values, interests, and abilities
- How values, interests, and abilities affect career choice
- How to help set up your career plan
- How to write an action plan to accomplish each objective.

Write Your Autobiography

Once you have created your space and started two portfolios, complete the next activities. They will help you analyze your talents and create your portfolio. Probably, one of the most helpful exercises you can do to examine your talents is to write your autobiography. I learned a great deal from writing mine several years ago. (See sidebar for more explanation.)

In the third area of your portfolio, titled "Autobiography," you should keep a ten-page autobiography. I suggest that you take a week and write your autobiography, at least a rough draft. By doing so, you will be able to look back at your life and see trends that will lead you to your new path. Although it may sound like a lot of work, writing your autobiography helps you to learn great tips about your own abilities and skills.

What Writing an Autobiography Taught Me

Dr. Margot B. Weinstein, CIPS

Until I went back to school to pursue a B.A. degree and wrote my autobiography, I had never realized the extent to which I had interviewed people, conducted research, and written lengthy documents and used them to help others. For example, I had written a book on my oldest son's journey through near fatal meningitis, one on my second son's severe head trauma caused by an abusive coach, and one on my father-in-law's journey into Alzheimer's disease, from onset until death. I had never published them formally, but they helped my family reach goals they would never have been able to reach without the research and the written works. I have always allowed others to publish on my research, but until writing my autobiography, I had never focused on those talents and how I could use them to build a new career path.

Since writing my autobiography, I have used my skills to build a flourishing business interviewing very successful people in different fields all over the world and writing, teaching, and speaking about their careers in organizations and schools worldwide as President and CEO of MW Leadership Consultants LLC.

We all have crises in life and challenges that change us. My feeling is if we learn about our talents—through writing an autobiography as I did or via some other avenue—we can use them in different ways to move up in a career. Remember, a career should not be only about your current job; it should also be a lifetime of loving what you do.

So that is what I mean when I urge you to write your autobiography. My hope is you will find something you did that will hit you, and you will say, "Oh, I have done that all my life in my career; I am good at that, and I can use it."

So, forget about grammar and spelling and just begin writing each day—two to three pages about your life. Discuss major issues—education, illness, family, clubs, awards—just allow yourself to be free to write whatever comes out. You can always edit it later, but start by getting your thoughts down on paper as they flow from your mind and heart.

Your autobiography will help you get in touch with:

- Your major jobs
- Your job highs and lows
- Trends you have repeated in life
- Activities you enjoy
- Important people in your life.

One activity that I have found can really help you get in touch with the factors that help you to write your autobiography is to do a timeline exercise where you divide all major issues in your life into five-year intervals from birth to your age today. You can either draw your career lifeline on a blank piece of paper or you can fill out the form on the next page to look at major factors in your life.

Place in each "five-year interval" box all the major aspects of your life such as:

- Year of your birth
- Birth of siblings
- Year of your marriage
- Any divorce or separation
- Deaths of people important to you

Activity: Timeline Exercise for Autobiography

0-5	5-10	10-15	15-20	20-25	25-30	30-35	35-40	40-45	50-55	55+

- All your jobs/internships
- Illnesses of your close family members such as children, siblings, etc.
- Education, degrees, training, continuing education courses.

Once you have done that, go back and circle the following:

- The best job you have ever had
- The worst job you have had
- Where you took the greatest risk of your life
- Where you encountered your biggest obstacles that prevented you from getting the job you wanted.

Then review the things you circled, and look to see if there are any patterns over your life that you can learn from and use to move forward in your career.

Discover Yourself

Explore the following areas to discover yourself: your abilities and skills, your personality type, your values, life situation, and learning style. All these factors are part of your whole.

Ask yourself the following questions and write down the answers. If your answers are too long to fit into the provided space, feel free to write them in a journal instead.

What are five words that best describe you? Next to each word, write a few sentences about why that word describes you.

Activity: Five Words that Describe You

1. _____

2. _____

3. _____

4. _____

5. _____

Next, write what you'd want it to read on your tombstone to describe your career. Although this may make you feel depressed or uncomfortable, answer them anyway. Many people put off finding their perfect career and follow an easy path because they think they have many more years to find it. You need to answer these questions to get to the heart of your life's purpose and your most satisfying career—and also to remind yourself that your time is limited.

Activity: Describe Your Career Tombstone

What was my greatest accomplishment at work?	What was my greatest challenge at work?
What are two descriptive words that I would least want on my tombstone?	What are two descriptive words that I would most want on my tombstone?
What would I do if I had only one more year to live?	What did I love best about my work?

Activity: Learn Your Life Values

Number the following list of eighteen values in order of their importance to you. Afterward, go back and place a star for the value you think is the most important, and one next to the value you think is the least important to you.

__ A comfortable life (prosperity)

__ An exciting life

__ A sense of accomplishment

__ A world of beauty

__ Equality and opportunity for all

__ Family security

__ Freedom and independence

__ Friendship and companionship

__ Happiness

__ Inner harmony and peace

__ Mature love (sexual and spiritual intimacy)

__ National security and safety

__ Pleasure

__ Salvation from sin

__ Self-respect and self-esteem

__ Social recognition

__ Wisdom

__ World peace

Activity: Learn Your Personal Trait Values

Number the following list of seventeen values in order of their importance to you. Place a star next to the value that is the most important, and a star next to the least important one to you.

___ Ambitious (hard working)

___ Broadminded

___ Capable

___ Cheerful

___ Clean (neat, tidy)

___ Courageous

___ Courteous and polite

___ Creative and imaginative

___ Forgiving

___ Helpful

___ Honest

___ Independent

___ Intellectual

___ Logical

___ Loving

___ Obedient

___ Self-disciplined

Activity: Learn Your Career Values

Number these twenty values in order of their importance to
you. Place a star next to the value that is the most important,
and a star next to the least important one to you.

___ Being independent

___ Being physically active

___ Creating beauty

___ Creating ideas

___ Designing new systems

___ Experiencing variety

___ Exploring ideas

___ Following directions

___ Having fun

___ Having status

___ Helping people

___ Improving society

___ Making money

___ Making things

___ Organizing things

___ Security

___ Solitude or quiet

___ Taking responsibility

___ Taking risks

___ Working with people

Activity: Self-Awareness

Write down the five values that are most important to you.

1. _____

2. _____

3. _____

4. _____

5. _____

After you have completed these activities, take a few minutes to reflect on how satisfied you are that you are pursuing what you truly value in your career. By this time, you should be getting in touch with what you value and what you truly want to pursue in your career. Then you can move to the fourth area of your portfolio.

In the fourth area of your portfolio, titled "Awards and Licenses," you should keep all the awards or certificates of recognition that you have obtained in life—perhaps you earned an award in high school, or an award from members of your community. The purpose is to use what you have to further your own career. Everyone has earned something over a lifetime. Go back to childhood if you have to and discover your past awards. Put them into this section.

In the fifth area of your portfolio, titled "Philosophy and Professional Goals," you should keep a statement of your personal philosophy and a sheet containing your professional goals. You may want to develop this section after you read chapters six and seven. Some people need to develop their ideas about career goals, niches, and business plans before they really know what they stand for. However, it's up to you. If you want to write one paragraph at this point, simply answer the following question.

Activity: My Mission Is—What Do I Want to Stand For?

_____

_____

_____

_____

_____

_____

_____

_____

You want your career goals to fit into your context/organization and your environment in the world. Think of your career fit as three circles as pictured in the activity below. It is your identity, that of your organization/context, and how you fit into the work world.

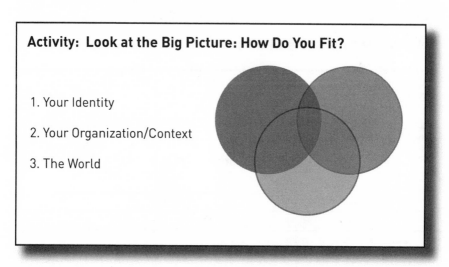

Activity: Look at the Big Picture: How Do You Fit?

1. Your Identity

2. Your Organization/Context

3. The World

Write one page in your journal with three paragraphs as if you were turning it into a professor at school. Use the following points:

1. List your ideal career field.

2. Discuss the types of organizations that offer careers in your field.

3. Identify general trends that are happening worldwide in your field, such as new opportunities, growth, downsizing, and out-sourcing. You always have to look at how you fit into what is happening in your field. Do not be specific. This is an overall picture just to get you thinking about the possibilities in your field and whether you are aligned with what is happening today.

In the next area of your portfolio, you should keep samples of your work. If you want to publish, and you have a copy of something you have written, place it in this section. If you want to be an artist or photographer, include your artwork. You get the idea. Next you should review your goals.

Activity: Set Your Goals with Timelines

Changes I want to make	Within the year	Within five years
1.		
2.		
3.		
4.		
5.		

One of the best activities I think you can do to move forward in your career journey is to make a contract with yourself and one other person. It should include a date and timelines. You can have someone sign it, or keep it as a record to review each new year to see if you completed your goals. Make them realistic. On the *Dr. Phil* show, he talks about learning contracts, and I have used them as a student and as a teacher. They are a wonderful way to help people stay on track. Complete the following activity to help you reach your goals.

Activity: Learning Contract

Write a one-page contract on how you will reach your goals.
If possible, have one other person sign it as a "witness."

1.   I want to reach the following goal.

2.   What resources do I need?

3.   What steps will I take next to reach the goal (with timeline)?

4.   How will I know that I have achieved this goal?

5.   How will I evaluate my achievement?

Your Signature and Date:

_____

(Your Witness) _____

Below is a list of the PROFESSIONAL GOALS that I wrote in 1998. I review them before each New Year, celebrate my accomplishments, and then rewrite a new plan after New Year's Eve. If I have completed my list from that year, even if I did not make all the money I wanted or it wasn't fulfilling, I celebrate the fact that I completed them. Not everything in life that you do will turn out to bring you what you envisioned, but the fact that you have gone after your dreams in a productive manner is worth celebrating.

My professional goals in 1998 were the following:

1. Interview successful people and write/teach/speak on strategies for success.
2. Consult with adults, children, and companies to provide solutions to career/life situations.
3. Write for four publications including professional papers, journals and books.
4. Present at two conferences in field per year.
5. Continue to learn by taking 2-3 courses formally each year.
6. Take two informal courses per year.
7. Be involved in three professional organizations.
8. Continue to work in real estate business.
9. Teach/mentor two students at college and university.
10. Stay healthy by balancing my life/work/family.

Interview with David Leeds

The next story is of my interview with **David Leeds**, who returned to college as he was approaching fifty, after having built a very success-ful career as a leader at Allstate. He returned to college for his B.A. at DePaul University, lost over seventy pounds, and after examining his life, has decided to pursue advanced degrees to become an adult educator when he retires from Allstate. This story illustrates how, by developing his portfolio and writing his autobiography, David was able to get in touch with his talents and dreams, and reach even higher career and personal goals. He even runs marathons. He is a true inspiration.

Background

I met David when he enrolled in the course I was teaching at DePaul University in 1999 titled "Learning Assessment Seminar." This is the first course students take when they return to college to get a Baccalaureate degree in the School for New Learning at DePaul University. At that time, David asked me to be his pro-fessional advisor and work with his senior academic advisor, Dr. Warren Scheideman at DePaul University. David wants to con-tinue his education to get a master's and a doctoral degree in or-der to teach other adult returning students when he retires from the workplace in his sixties.

Q: What is your position and career background at Allstate?

LEEDS: "I am now in a leadership role as a marketing manager in the insurance industry, and it is quite rewarding. I have been working my way up the ladder with Allstate for twelve years, which is the longest that I have been with any one industry and in one organization in my career life. I started out working as an underwriting assistant in one of the regional offices thirteen years ago. I have worked hard, and I have had many promotions."

Keep Your Career Information

Q: Did you always keep your career information?

LEEDS: "Yes. I had all of my materials, books, and journals in boxes that I dragged around the country with my moves for years, but the information in the boxes was not organized."

Q: Why did you return to college at almost age fifty?

LEEDS: "In late 1999, I moved to Chicago after I received the biggest promotion of my life. I had been working in corporate America for nearly ten years at that time, and I needed that piece of paper that showed I had a college degree to continue to move up. I knew that I have a bright future at Allstate, but without the piece of paper from a university I am not a member of the club and I will not be able to reach my full potential. It has been over four years since I started, and I am still working on that degree, but it is not elusive anymore. With another little push, I will have it within the year.

In addition, I knew that in order to become more professional and organize myself in the final stage in my life near fifty, I wanted my degree. I found the program at DePaul University. And one of the first things that they have you do at DePaul is take the 'Learning Assessment Seminar.' With you as my professor, I wrote my autobiography as part of the course requirement as well as doing many career exercises toward building a portfolio."

Q: Had you ever written your autobiography or organized your career information before entering the course with me at DePaul?

LEEDS: "No, nothing other than a résumé, which is only a very small part of your business career. Periodically, I would review my background to check and see what would make myself better—to retool myself. Throughout my career I have always found that the best way to do that was to see what I needed and not be afraid to go and seek that. So while I ended up leaving school at a young age and not getting my degree, I never stopped assessing myself, and taking inventories of what skills I was lacking and how to get them."

Q: How did you begin to organize the information to write your autobiography?

LEEDS: "At forty-nine, I began by organizing the material that I had always kept in the boxes. I spent several weekends sorting and piling, but not throwing anything away so that I could utilize all of my past experiences. It was very difficult to write my autobiography and put together a portfolio. I had to review information that I had kept for over thirty years, since graduating high school. So the task was not easy, but I realized that there had been a reason that I had dragged all my information around in boxes for years."

Lessons Learned

Q: Did organizing your career information and writing your autobiography help you move forward?

LEEDS: "Absolutely. When I organized my information to write a reflective autobiography—which as you remember was titled 'Becoming the Director of My Dreams'—I learned so many things:

1. *Channel My Talents.* I was able to funnel down the information to a point where I could channel it. Writing my biography forced me to focus on the qualities that I knew were innate, but that I was not using to their full extent. For example, I found a note from one of my high school teachers that praised me for being an exceptional organizer. In addition, I found notes in my old yearbooks that made me realize that I had survived

several career crises, including one at age forty-two when I moved from one relatively successful career to a whole new career in corporate America, working with computers. I had no formal training and had to go in and prove myself from the ground floor up. I was able to use the insight that I gained from organizing the information to capitalize on these skills and qualities to move my autobiography forward.

2. *Gain Confidence.* I learned that you can go places faster once you get started because you gain confidence and energy from the experience. I started out with small steps in school. The very first class that I took at DePaul was hard for me, but now that I am in motion, it is easier to continue to move forward with my goals—taking more than one course a semester and fitting them into my already busy schedule.

3. *Find Transcripts.* Developing my autobiography and portfolio forced me to find my old college transcripts for courses that I taken thirty-five years ago. Many of these courses were transferable into DePaul's program, and so I got credit for things that I had already done that were meaningful to me at the time that I did them. To a lot of institutions that would not have mattered, but that all counted in DePaul's program.

4. *Write Essays for College Credit.* I was able to earn additional college credit by writing papers in which I reflected on my past experiences—like my trip in 1990 to Europe with my mom—and gained new insight into them. In the School for

New Learning you can use your life experiences to write essays for college credit if you can document the information properly—which, as my advisor, you know that I have been able to do—and show via a reflective paper that you have learned from them.

5. *Insights Into My Ideal Career.* It made me realize what I wanted to ultimately do in my career. I realized that I wanted to become a teacher upon retirement from Allstate, to train or retrain other returning adult students. And I knew at that point I wanted to get my degree in adult education. So I refocused with my biography as a background on how I could obtain my B.A., M.A. and Ed.D. in adult and continuing education. At this time, I feel very self-motivated to do new things, and I want to accomplish these achievements so that I can give back and teach other returning adults. So it became very important for me to redesign my plans to reach my next level, one in which I want to give back by helping others reach their goals.

6. *Balance My Life.* I realized that I could be successful in several aspects of my life at the same time. I am now able to do the program at DePaul while simultaneously pursuing a rewarding career at Allstate. Before organizing my material, it had been a struggle to juggle every aspect of my life successfully. Writing my autobiography was the kickoff of saying, 'Yes, I can have a rewarding career, get a degree, and pursue my dreams both in

my career and personal life all at the same time.' I learned that it is just a matter of reorganizing yourself, redirecting, and taking past experiences and building on them.

7. *Focus on My Dreams.* Organizing my information has been instrumental in keeping me focused on my dreams and using my skills and abilities to their fullest. I now see that my dream is within reach. And with every month and quarter that goes by, I am closer to it, whether I am writing papers or attending classes. Without doing these exercises and putting them into focus, I would have just stagnated. I would have just been walking around the same stretch of sand for the rest of my life. But I wanted to find a new boardwalk, and by reflecting on my past, I got new insight to plan for my future and move forward."

Q: You have lost over seventy pounds since I have known you and you have been able to keep it off for more than a year. Did organizing your material and examining your past have any effect on your deciding to lose weight?

LEEDS: "Yes. Losing weight is all about self-determination. And by organizing my thoughts through writing my autobiography and creating a portfolio, I was able to gain some kind of inner strength that I could call upon to accomplish this goal. Until completing these exercises, I had not contemplated a weight loss program. As I analyzed my life, I realized that my weight had become a detriment to my well-being. I was uncomfortable flying. I was uncomfortable walking. My joints hurt. And I wanted to do something about it. And so I learned how to capitalize on my past skills by going back and doing two things: (1) I explored the different options that I had from an educational perspective, asking myself, 'What is the best way to do this for myself?' And, (2) I had to call upon the reserves of willpower and strength to get through the program and stay with the program long-term. And, in fact, I still go to my meetings every week, even though I do not need to by way of the requirements of the program. I do it for the requirements of David. I have lost in the range of seventy-five pounds; I had never lost that much before and successfully kept it off for more than one year. I have now accomplished that."

Advice on Success from David

Q: Would you advise others who want to move up in their careers to do a portfolio and write their autobiography?

LEEDS: "Absolutely. Do a portfolio. Do an autobiography. Do a vitae or a résumé. All of those things together give you a history of who you are so that you can move forward. These are excellent tools to help hone and guide you to find your best approach to learning as an adult. It will help you realize how you dealt with self-defining moments in your life. The process may be very emotional, or even very distressing, but if you organize your information in an autobiography and a portfolio, you can maintain functionality through future crises and through life changes to use your past to move forward both personally and professionally. You will be able to reflect on your past moments of truth that have affected you at certain points in your life. Then, you will be able to use them to keep moving forward by putting one foot in front of the other so that you can conquer them to reach your goals.

"It may not be easy. It may seem overwhelming to take this new step. Do not think that just because you get organized, it will be easy for you to leap forward with both feet. Sometimes you may need to take a baby step to get started, but once you are into it, the floodgates will be loosened, and you will see how you can successfully reach another level in your life. Then, you too can be the 'Director of Your Dreams.'"

Author's Concluding Tips

In summary, it may seem overwhelming to do these exercises to develop a portfolio; on paper it will appear to you it takes much more time to do this than to focus on subjects in other chapters of this book, but you need to do the work to move forward. A portfolio is valuable both to learn about yourself and to use to obtain work. You may need to be with others to develop one instead of by yourself. If you need to work with others, then by all means, sign up for a course or a workshop. You can visit my Web site to learn about the workshops I often give at organizations and universities. Also, many colleges offer portfolio development advice via seminars, workshops, and courses.

Step 3: Learn About the Field

Interview with Jennifer Ames

"ENJOY THE JOURNEY"

7. Work Hard and Leverage Each Job to Create Your Perfect Career!

6. Put Plan into Action

5. Start a Career Plan

4. Educate Yourself

3. Learn About the Field

2. Examine Your Talents

1. Organize

Drawing by Phil Orlandi

Chapter Three
Step 3: Learn About the Field

"After analyzing my abilities and lifestyle goals, I realized that my parents were right: Real estate was a perfect fit for me for many reasons."
—Jennifer Ames

Points to Remember

➢ Network, network, and network: Talk with family, friends, and anyone you meet who works in a field that interests you.

➢ Do research on the Internet.

➢ Read professional publications.

➢ Attend seminars and conferences.

➢ Join professional organizations in the field.

➢ Volunteer.

➢ Take internships or part-time or full-time positions.

➢ Interview people in the field.

There are many ways for you learn about fields that might contain your potential new career. This chapter discusses several ways to approach finding out about them. When you were exploring your talents and abilities, chances are that several potential career fields presented themselves. Most people have some inkling of what they are interested in or suited for, and the examination we discussed in chapter two should either confirm that feeling or send you off in a completely new direction. The point of this chapter is to give you some guidelines for exploring the one or two fields you've probably settled on by now. Just take this advice one field at a time. This is the fun part—and it can be very informative!

Network, Network, and Network

I cannot stress strongly enough the importance of using your relationships. People often undervalue their personal contacts as networking opportunities. In fact, they often fail to realize how valuable it is to network at all. Sit down and write out a list of family members, friends, and business contacts who may be able to guide or support you. Then, contact them and make them aware of your current status. If you run into a friend who is now working in a field that interests you, be sure to let him know. You may want to ask him some questions about the field, good companies to work for, available jobs, and whether he or she knows anyone who could help you. People are often flattered when you take an interest in their work, as long as you are not too pushy. You might say, "Oh, that sounds interesting, perhaps something I would enjoy being involved in. Do you have any suggestions for how I could learn about the field?"

Do Research on the Internet

Use the Internet to do research in your field. Today, you need only a PC and a modem to do research on your field, no matter where you are around the world. You can do this research while on vacation in the islands, from your home, or from an office. You can learn a wealth of information about your field, as well as about companies, available jobs, and business trends. Ironically, the sheer wealth of available information can actually confuse you further! To avoid this fate, I offer two suggestions:

1. *Stay Focused.* Organize your search around specific objectives. Resist the temptation to just browse when the spirit moves you. I suggest you make a list of the types of information you are looking for, and then go on a search engine and stay with the topic.

2. *Learn How to Access the Information.* Web sites are organized sequentially. Someone once said to me that a Web site is designed like a tree, with each branch leading to five or six other branches (or levels of information). At first you may be confused about this and have to backtrack, but if you stay with it you will get better at accessing the organization of Web site material. Practice makes perfect.

Read Professional Publications

You can go to a library or bookstores, or you can buy subscriptions to newspapers and trade papers. I have found that once you have chosen a field, professional trade magazines and books such as *CRAIN'S Chicago Business, Midwest Real Estate News, Affordable Housing Magazine,* and *Chicago REALTOR®* will provide you with the best information and career opportunities. What better way to learn about the intricacies of a career in the affordable housing industry than to subscribe to *Affordable Housing Magazine*?

Attend Seminars and Conferences

You will learn and meet valuable contacts at the same time. If you subscribe to the professional trade magazines, you will be able to read about upcoming events in your area. You can register for most conferences online or through fax and telephone. They are often not restricted for just members of a profession or people in the field, but always check first before giving your credit card information. Once you are at a seminar or conference, make the most of it by talking with people and giving out your business cards. Also, pay attention, listen, and take notes at the sessions. Put all the information in a folder in your "Career Central" after the conference.

Join Professional Organizations

Today, almost every field has accredited professional organizations. I suggest that you find out which ones are located in your area, and attend a few meetings. If you enjoy the meetings, join and get involved. Once you are involved you will meet people who can help you, build your résumé, and get some valuable experience at working on different tasks in your field. Again, many organizations will let you attend as a guest without being part of the profession, but I would always contact them first to make sure it is okay.

Volunteer

Volunteering is always a terrific way to learn. If you do not have a lot of time, you can offer to volunteer at an event or on a limited basis. Make it clear to people at the organizations that you want to be involved, but you do not have a great deal of free time—and perhaps money—to be at all the events. For example, I offered to co-head a "Building Your Business" forum for the American Society of Training and Development (CC-ASTD), although I am not on CC-ASTD's Board. This has given me a chance to build my business, learn a great deal, and network without going to meetings every month. I also participate in several events and write for the Chicago Association of REALTORS® (CAR) on several areas that are close to my heart. I sponsored an essay contest and participated in Mayor Daley's "Principal for a Day" Program by sponsoring children at Inter-American Magnet School at the same time.

Take an Internship or Part-time or Full-time Position

If you have an opportunity to take a part-time or full-time position in your field while continuing your regular work, I suggest you do so. Internships are not just for college students. Sometimes, you can take an unpaid position at a company as a learning experience. This is a valid way for adults to learn about a field and (who knows?) it could turn into a full-time PAID job at a later date.

It may be very difficult to balance everything in the beginning, but it is easier to find a career you want once you are working in the field. However, I do realize that most people cannot afford to quit their day job to pursue their dreams. I went back to school while still working in property management and development, and my children were not grown at the time. The sacrifices were worth it.

Interview People in the Field

This is a terrific way to find out what others like and dislike about working in your desired field. As I went through my four degrees, I always interviewed people whom I thought had a job I would like. I was always honest with them about that, and they were always willing to share information about their job. Consequently, I was able to learn about and stay away from many jobs that would not have fit my talents and personality. Some ways to go about that are listed in the next activity.

Then, reflect on the interview, and always ask yourself how the story ties to you. Personal interviews are a wonderful way to learn about a field. In my opinion, they present a more accurate picture than reading a thousand articles.

Complete the activity sheet on the next page to create a plan for learning about your field.

Activity: Choose someone to interview in the field and ask the following questions:

1. How did you find your career?

2. Why did you choose your field?

3. How did you become successful?

4. What obstacles did you have to overcome?

5. What training/education did you need?

6. What advice would you offer others who want to follow in your path?

Activity: My Thirty-day Plan

1. List three people I can contact to ask about my field.

2. What are names of two organizations I can research online?

3. I want to interview the following person in the next month.

4. I will attend the following conference(s) in the next month.

Interview with Jennifer Ames

The next interview is from top real-estate sales professional Jennifer Ames. Jennifer is a Yale graduate who, after working in two other fields, chose to enter real estate sales. This story illustrates how important it is for you to use all your contacts to learn about different career paths that will fit your unique talents and abilities. Often, those close to you will provide you with valuable information you can use to find the field that's right for you.

Biography

For the last six years, **Jennifer Ames** has ranked in the top ten agents out of all the agents in the city of Chicago, based on her total closed sales volume. She graduated from Yale University in 1983 with a B.A. in English Literature. Prior to her career in real estate, Jennifer worked as an investment banker and then as a film producer. She went into the real estate business in 1994. She has been quoted as an expert in her field by the *Chicago Tribune, The Wall Street Journal, Crain's Chicago Business*, and other industry publications. She has also appeared on *Fox Thing in the Morning*, CLTV, and CNN. Jennifer's business is largely based on referrals from past clients and includes buyers and sellers with a diverse range of needs and price points. In 1994, her first year in residential real estate sales,

Jennifer outperformed her peers and was recognized as the company's "Rookie of the Year." In subsequent years, she has consistently received the industry's most prestigious awards, including the Chicago Association of REALTORS® Bronze, Silver, and Golden Eagle Awards. She has ranked among the top ten agents in Chicago out of several thousand every year since 1997. In 2003, Jennifer sold in excess of $60 million in residential real estate. In 2004, Jennifer was also featured on the front page of the magazine by the National Association of REALTORS® as one of the top agents nationwide.

Learn from Other Job Experiences

Q: When you graduated from Yale, you first worked in investment banking. Why did you choose that as a career path?

AMES: "I started working part-time in investment banking and public finance in 1981, during summer vacation from college. I worked the next two summers as well, and then came back to investment banking full-time from 1984 to 1989. My clients were state universities and municipal governments. I entered the field because I wanted to do something in public service. Giving back to the community has been a common theme in my career path. I have always pursued career opportunities where there was a feel-good component and where I believed I was helping people. At the end of the day, it is important to feel that my work directly affects people's lives in a positive manner. I work really hard in my career, and believe there needs to be a sense of accomplishing something more than simply earning money."

Q: What made you ultimately decide that investment banking was not a perfect career fit for you?

AMES: "Investment banking in the 1980s was still a very difficult place for women. This reality was reflected in compensation and promotion policies. My employer offered a benefit plan that was really geared toward rewarding longevity. For women who were thinking about having children at some point, this did not really work. I watched the career of a colleague, one of the few women in my department, get derailed within six weeks of when she let the company know of her pregnancy. Her colleagues were not at all supportive and felt that her pregnancy was a betrayal of her commitment to the firm. So, although I was single, I knew that I wanted children in the future, and I was concerned about working in an environment that was so unsupportive of women professionals."

Q: Your second career path was as a partner in a film production company. Explain why you selected that as a career path and why it ended up not being right for you.

AMES: "I enjoyed working as a producer in the film business. This was a good next step because it allowed me to have the independence I was looking for and to express my creative side. However, what I found after about three and a half years was that I did not share my business partner's vision of how to run a business. He was a creative genius but not a practical person. He would go way over budget on fixed-price projects and, at the end of the day, it would become my problem to deal with. Since I wasn't able to print money, it was hard for me to take from Peter to pay Paul. I really did enjoy our work, but it grew increasingly uncomfortable working with my business partner. I felt that my reputation was being compromised. Above all else, I value my professional reputation. I also realized how much I wanted to control my destiny. So I knew this career was not a perfect fit for me."

Learn from People Close to You

Q: Even though you could have chosen many fields that required more education, you chose real estate. What made you consider this field?

AMES: "All of my family members, especially my parents, encouraged me to pursue a career in real estate. My family has been involved with residential real estate development and sales in Chicago since the late 1800s. My great grandfather was involved in early development in the city's Gold Coast. My stepfather's family started Sudler and Company in the 1920s, and were actively involved in sales, management, and development until the company was sold in 1989. My mother sold residential real estate for thirty years, and my dad is currently taking a leadership role in the preservation of large farms in New England."

Find a Role Model

Q: Your mother was really your primary role model and she also believed that real estate was a perfect fit for you. Why?

AMES: "My mother strongly encouraged me to pursue real estate as a career because she understood my strengths, my skills, and my personality. She recognized that real estate would be a good career path for me before I saw it for myself, for the following reasons:

- She thought it would be a good fit based on my outgoing personality.
- She also has a strong belief in the importance of giving back to the community, and we share the belief that real estate transactions strongly affect people's lives.
- She knew that at some point I wanted to have my own family and real estate is a female-dominated field that's more flexible in terms of childbearing schedules.
- She saw it as a field where I could use my established business and civic connections to excel."

Learn by Reading in Your Field

Q: Other than your family members, did anyone else also influence your career path?

AMES: "Yes. I was really inspired by the book, *Use What You've Got, and Other Business Lessons I've Learned from My Mom*, by dynamo Barbara Corcoran, founder of the Corcoran Group in New York. Her entire book is about her career success. Barbara goes through different things she learned from her mother and from growing up in a large family. She recounts events in her life, and how she later applied those to her professional career. I found her story fascinating because she is a little bit like me. There were things that she learned along the way—really important lessons that helped shape her success. When I was in New York this year, I met with Barbara Corcoran. She has done an amazing job of bringing her company to a new level of professionalism and customer service in the industry. Her organization has minimum standards for marketing and customer service that the agents are required to deliver. I think it is really important because they have established a company where the entire organization is known for a high level of quality."

Match Your Talents with the Field

Q: Ultimately, what did you learn about yourself and the industry that made you realize that real estate sales was your ideal career?

AMES: "After analyzing my abilities and lifestyle goals, I realized that real estate was a perfect fit for me for many reasons:

1. *I Can Control My Time and Decisions.* I wanted to have total control of my time and my business decisions. I believed in myself, and I knew that I would have the discipline to put everything into my business that it would take to be successful. I did not want somebody else setting arbitrary rules about the hours I worked or telling me that I cannot take a vacation. I work hard and play hard. Taking time out occasionally is important for one's soul. I was looking for a career that allowed me the opportunity to travel. Since I started selling real estate, I have explored remote parts of China, fly fished north of the Arctic circle, celebrated Christmas in Bali, Fiji, and St. Lucia, honeymooned in South Africa, and climbed Mt. Kilimanjaro—Africa's highest mountain.

2. *I Can Control My Earnings.* I wanted to work in a non-political environment where my earnings would be based solely on the time and effort I invested. I did not want a career where my compensation was influenced by other people's successes and failures. When I was in investment banking, there were years when my department exceeded our goals but our bonuses were reduced to subsidize other departments that were less successful. That is a tough pill to swallow when your year-end bonus

is more than 50 percent of your total compensation. You had a lot at risk each year. Since I went into real estate, I have worked very hard and consistently exceeded my prior year's income.

3. *I Can Protect My Professional Reputation.* I have always valued my professional reputation, and was a little hesitant to go into real estate because it wasn't a particularly sophisticated industry. Unfortunately, there are many part-timers in real estate looking for a little extra spending money, and people's impressions of real estate people are influenced by our lowest common denominator. However, I quickly realized that I could turn that problem into an advantage. With my education and prior career history, I had an opportunity to create a new image as a real estate salesperson. By utilizing my skills, I became a leader. To this day, I continually refine and improve the quality of the services I offer my clients. As a result, my business is diverse, and has grown to include significant market share within the high-end, luxury market.

4. *I Can Provide Superior Customer Service.* I like being in a field where in order to succeed I have to provide top customer service. (Of course, this is true in many careers.) I enjoy working hard to understand my clients' needs and issues, and working with them to resolve problems. I have been able to utilize the skills that I developed in my other careers:

   • *Using a Team Approach.* I have a full-time assistant in my office to do my scheduling and keep abreast of properties on the market. I work well with other professionals to ensure that deals close smoothly.

- *Doing Research.* I try to learn the issues and uniqueness of each deal to resolve problems and ensure success. I share that information with my clients.

- *Being a Resource for My Clients.* I offer support, services, and information to my clients from the beginning of a deal and stay involved through closing to ensure that everything progresses smoothly. I negotiate as a team player with everyone to ensure a smooth transaction. Perhaps most important, I take a long-term view of the relationship, and recommend only what is in my clients' best interest.

5. *I Am Able to Continue Learning.* I am able to learn from other top professionals in my field as well as professionals in other fields through conferences, training programs, and professional relationships. For example, I continue to receive training at Coldwell Banker on current topics in business. I attend conferences and lectures at Coldwell Banker's President's Club yearly. I keep up with changes in business such as new technologies. I think that technology is changing many fields, and professionals must stay current. Today, I use a handheld computer to manage my schedule, maintain a database of other agents, keep track of my deals, and stay in touch with clients. Also, I believe in constantly learning to improve my services. I take a few minutes each day to think about how I can more effectively perform my job.

I continue to improve the level of professionalism that I offer my clients by being efficient and detail-oriented. I've been selling for ten years, but the way I transact business is still evolving.

6. *I Can Give Back to My Community.* I wanted a field where I felt that I was providing a service to people, a field that has a positive influence in other people's lives. One's home is such a critical part of life, and I help people find exactly the right home, location, etc. Helping someone find and purchase a home is a sacred trust, because that is where they'll raise their children, plant their gardens, retreat from the storms of life, etc. I believe in building relationships, and I never manipulate people to steer them to the home I am trying to sell, but I try to genuinely work hard to make sure they end up in the home that is right for them.

7. *Freedom to Create a Balanced Life.* I wanted a career where I could have freedom to create what I feel is a balanced life. From many people's perspective, my life isn't balanced, because I work most of my waking hours. But from my perspective, it is fine because I have an opportunity to do everything that I value. I enjoy my career and find it very fulfilling. But I also sneak in quality time with my husband, my family, and my friends, and I make time to travel."

Advice from Jennifer for You

Q: What advice can you offer others who are trying to select a field?

AMES: "I think that in order for you to choose a career that is perfect for you, you must select a field were you can:

1. *Be Passionate About What You Do.* I think the most important factor in career success is for you to choose a field in which you really love what you do. In my opinion, you cannot be focused and work the number of hours it takes to be really successful if you are not passionate about the work. If you look at the number of hours that I work (and it's not just hours sitting at a desk or meeting with clients), I am always thinking about my work. Even when I'm falling asleep or waking up, new ideas are coming into my head; I am always interested in the intellectual challenge of how I can improve what I am doing, and that is, to me, an important part of being successful.

2. *Be Professional.* I believe that a good professional reputation is essential today. Therefore, choose a field and/or an organization where you feel you can build a professional reputation, and where your values are not in conflict with those who pay your check.

3. *Enjoy Fair Financial Compensation.* It is important to make sure that your career is compatible with your lifestyle. Although I had interests in a number of potential careers, I ultimately selected one that had significant potential to support the lifestyle I wanted for myself. Having said that, I plunged right in and didn't worry about my income. I had confidence that if I worked hard, it would follow. And it did.

4. *Have Control, Freedom, and Independence.* You should think about where, when, and how you like to work. Some people want structure, some people don't. My preference was to find a career that gave me the freedom to choose my projects, to travel, and to work from home. I chose real estate not only because I could build my own organization with my own values, but I could also be successful working at my chosen destination and setting my own schedule.

5. *Continue to Learn.* I do not believe in being complacent in any field. Know that part of success in your career in any field will be for you to love learning about the business so that you can improve how you work. Do not select a field in which you will be bored learning new facets of the business.

6. *Value Relationships.* You should choose a field where you can build on relationships with people from your family and your community, with colleagues, co-workers, and clients.

7. *Stay Healthy.* You should try to select a career where you can incorporate factors to build a healthy lifestyle. I now carry healthy snacks with me all day, and I hired a trainer to make sure that I get proper exercise daily. Also, you should think about where your office will be located so that it is convenient for your lifestyle. If I had a two-hour commute every day I might not have time to exercise."

Q: Do you have a philosophy that guides your career?

AMES: "Yes. Whatever your career choice, set your sights high and keep pushing yourself to do better. Early in my career, somebody told me that if you set your goal to do $5 million in sales, you may accomplish that goal. And if you set your goal to do $50 million in sales, you may accomplish that goal. But if you set your sights on $5 million in sales, it is highly unlikely you will sell $50 million. Each year, I raise the bar for myself by setting realistic, but higher goals. Then I challenge myself and my team to discover how we can reach them."

Author's Concluding Tip

In closing, do not underestimate the value of learning from your family members and people close to you. Although Jennifer Ames tried other fields, her parents and family members suggested she try real estate because they understood the field and her talents, and real estate ended up being her perfect career. The field that is right for you may be closer than you think.

Step 4: Educate Yourself in Your Field: It's Never Too Late

Interview with Shandra Findley & Nancy Suvarnamani

"ENJOY THE JOURNEY"

7. Work Hard and Leverage Each Job to Create Your Perfect Career!

6. Put Plan into Action

5. Start a Career Plan

4. Educate Yourself

3. Learn About the Field

2. Examine Your Talents

1. Organize

Drawing by Phil Orlandi

Chapter Four

Step 4: Educate Yourself in Your Field: It's Never Too Late

"College is not always necessary in many fields to earn a great amount of money, but you need an education to be successful, professional, and confident in business and in teaching." **—Shandra Findley**

"The opportunities for everyone to receive an education— whether it is a designation, training, continuing education, license, or a college degree—are endless in America." **—Nancy Suvarnamani**

Points to Remember

➢ Enroll in training programs.

➢ Take professional development courses.

➢ Pursue continuing education courses.

➢ Acquire license or state certification (if required).

➢ Obtain professional designations.

➢ Get college or advanced degrees (if required).

➢ Keep copies of all educational/training certificates or transcripts.

➢ Set fear aside or find help.

After you have discovered your talents and learned about your field, the next step is to find out how much training and education it takes to be successful in that career. Today, due to constant changes in the workplaces and advances in technology, more and more education is being required to enter a field and then to maintain adequate knowledge, licenses, and certifications. Richard Nelson Bolles (2004), in his new addition of *What Color Is Your Parachute: A Practical Manual for Job-hunters and Career Changes*, says, "Chances are on a job interview, you have received the bad news. It goes something like: 'In order to be hired for this job, you have to have a master's degree and ten years' experience.'" Bolles adds, "There are always exceptions to every rule, except where a profession has a rigid entrance examination, as in, say, medicine or law." (p. 200).

I agree that there are always exceptions, but do not interpret this to mean that you can just dive right into a new profession without preparation. You wouldn't want your hairdresser to highlight your hair or your bus driver to walk in off the street and start driving you around the city without the proper training, would you? Would you want a surgeon to operate on you or a lawyer to represent you without the proper license, training, and education—get the connection? So you need to find out what the requirements are in your field, and then get the education that is required, plus whatever level you need to be successful and maintain professionalism. More often than not, it is the combination of education and practice that helps make the successful person. In chapter two, I told you about David Leeds who had returned to college at fifty to get a degree in order to reach a higher leadership level in his organization. In this chapter you will meet Shandra Findley, who returned to college for a B.A. degree while working full-time as a teacher and raising six children. The point is simply this: No one is too old to get an education or a degree. You just have to discover the requirements in your field, know your talents, and find an education program that will match your needs—and then, of course, take the time, do the work, and be determined to complete the program!

All types of education can be extremely beneficial to you. Your dream career may not require formal certificates or degrees, but rather participation in training programs, professional development courses, continuing education courses, seminars, conferences, or workshops. Often, you can get designations or certificates to move up in your field. In real estate, for example, you can obtain designations that are recognized around the world. Sometimes degrees, including master's and doctorate degrees, are necessary. Whatever your field requires, you should obtain them.

Begin to learn about the education programs available in your field, and put one of them on your to do list. You will learn great information, get needed credentials, gain new skills, meet people in your field, and hopefully have a great time in the process.

Pursue Continuing Education Courses

Learning has the power to transform you and help you become more successful, and a major part of doing an exceptional job is your ability to learn. A commitment to be a lifelong learner is a critical component in your successful career because during the last century we have moved from the Industrial Age through the Information Age to the Knowledge Age. You must have the ability to obtain, assimilate, and apply the right knowledge effectively. Your ability will no longer be judged solely by qualifications gained in the past, but will also be judged by your capacity to learn and adapt in the future.

1. *Learning can*:
   - Help you be more financially successful
   - Help you achieve your full potential (You have the ability to learn throughout your life in all types of surroundings at home, at work, at play.)
   - Help you solve complex problems
   - Help you change your attitude
   - Make you more interesting to be with
   - Be fun
   - Be very challenging.

If you decide you love to learn, you can learn anywhere, with family, friends, walking your dog, playing sports—it is endless.

2. *Many factors can affect your learning*:
   - Your motivation
   - Your preferred learning styles
   - Your opportunities to the use information

- Demands that life makes on your time
- Your resources
- Your self-image of learning
- Rewards associated with any learning activity
- Availability of learning opportunities
- Availability of appropriate learning environments
- The climate in which your learning takes place.

Our society is rapidly changing into a knowledge and information society. You must make a commitment to continue to be successful regardless of your field. Just think of how new technologies are quickly changing most businesses throughout the world, and making information accessible to most people in a 24/7 environment.

Acquire License or State Certifications (If Required)

As I said earlier, I am sure that you want to go only to licensed people in many fields: medicine, law, and, in my opinion, real estate. So if you want to learn what your field requires, your first step might be to visit the government site in your state and learn what is required. Then, you can work on finding how you can receive it.

Obtain Professional Designations

In many fields, you can earn designations that will add value to your career. In teaching, real estate, training, and human resource development there are several accredited designations you can pursue that are recognized and valued across the industry. Many are offered through accredited institutions online, so you may not even have to leave your house or change out of your pajamas to receive the education. However, if you do attend classes like the second interviewee in this chapter, Nancy Suvarnamani, you will receive the added benefit of meeting a terrific network of professionals face-to-face and making friends with professors and other students taking the program. Even if you have to take time off to attend courses, it will be worth the effort and sacrifice.

Get College or Advanced Degrees (If Required)

A college degree will often provide you the necessary credentials, credibility, skills, and self-esteem to pursue your dream career. Most important, according to the *Princeton Review*, you will earn more money than without one—at least $28,000 per year more. And in many fields, going to the right college will allow you to start off with a salary double what you would earn without a degree. In addition, Richard Nelson Bolles, in his popular career book of 1995, *What Color Is Your Parachute: A Practical Manual for Job-hunters and Career Changes*, points out that "many students of all ages get their internships through college programs, and one out of seven students in some sections of the country get an internship or a job placement from the school" (p. 428).

Colleges have degree programs that are designed and accessible for people of all ages with all different types of needs. Many degrees are offered completely online, and several colleges offer programs that you can go through as a group so that you have the same classmates through the entire program. One thing I would stress is that you need to go to a school that is accredited both as an institution and in the program you selected. It is even better if the school is recognized as a top school by sources like the *Princeton Review*. But, aside from that advice, do not let going back to school for a certificate or degree stand in the way of your dreams: There is a college and a program that is right for you.

I returned to school in my forties, and received my baccalaureate, two master's degrees, and my doctorate in seven and a half years, while working part-time and raising my family. It wasn't easy, but it was well worth it. I now mentor and counsel students who return to college and all of them find it difficult, but the knowledge they gain opens doors for them, and most importantly, they gain a sense of self-esteem and confidence that is priceless. They always tell me at the end that it was well worth the struggle. A woman who lived in my apartment building returned to college after raising her children and became a pediatric surgeon at the well-known Children's Memorial Hospital in Chicago. So today, anything is possible. I believe in the value of learning. In the words of Albert Einstein, "Never regard study as a duty, but as the enviable opportunity to learn to know the liberating influence of beauty in the realm of the spirit for your own personal joy and to the profit of the community to which your later work belongs."

Activity: My Plan to Get My Education/Degree/License

What type of education/ degree do I need?	How am I going to get it?	Where will I pursue it?	When will I pursue it?	When do I expect to complete it?

Keep Copies of All Education/Training Certificates or Transcripts

As I said in chapter two in "Portfolio Development," I learned when counseling adults that many adults have taken education/training through their workplaces or through volunteer activities that they have no records in their portfolio. Whether you have lost certificates, or never had them because you took them so long ago that you have forgotten about them, I advise you to obtain records of all programs or courses you have completed. If you do not have them, go back and try to get copies. You can use the form in chapter two to document what transcripts or certificates you need and where to get copies of them. It doesn't matter whether your workplace demanded you complete a course, or you chose to take it, you need to use it to your advantage. Using the Web is a wonderful method for contacting an organization or school to see how/where/when/how much it will cost you to get copies or certificates of completion. In addition, if possible, get a list of courses and an explanation of what was taught in each. Then, you can use that information in a job interview or your portfolio. All types of education, training courses, and programs will add value to your knowledge base and help you build a portfolio.

Set Fear Aside or Find Help

Do not let fear prevent you from going after the education you need to pursue your dream career. Whether you are short on time or have financial or family difficulties or childcare issues, as the old saying goes, "Where there is a will, there is a way." Today, there are many outstanding accredited programs, both traditional and online, as well as wonderful programs specifically designed for the adult student. The School of New Learning at DePaul University and Adult and Continuing Education at Northern Illinois University are prime examples. These universities are designed to help returning adult students.

Hopefully, by reading the story of the next interviewee, Shandra Findley, who returned to school as a mother of six children, and Nancy Suvarnamani, who came to the United States from Thailand to get advanced degrees, you will see that you are never too old to pursue an education. There are also many books on the subject available through Amazon.com, such as *Study Skills for Adults Returning to School* by Jerold W. Apps and *Returning to Learning: Studying as an Adult: Tips, Traps and Triumphs* by Caroline Brem.

There are also many study guides available online, through bookstores and at universities, on how to succeed as a returning adult student. In addition, there are many adult counselors, such as myself, who advise students on how to be successful at school. Some of the subjects that are regularly discussed when I counsel adult students are:

- Receiving financial support services
- Learning about child care or elder care issues
- Practicing motivational techniques

- Developing learning/memory techniques

- Improving reading skills

- Taking notes and outlining

- Using personal learning styles

- Learning how to study

- Learning to take tests

- Learning time management

- Using learning resources

- Developing organizational strategies

- Evaluating professors and their teaching styles

- Using the computer and new technologies for school.

So set aside any fears you may have. You can solve most school issues and be successful if you want to badly enough. Determination and hard work go a long way. I received four college degrees in seven and a half years, including my doctorate with honors, and I believe firmly that although you must have the skills, it is more important that you want it badly and are willing to work hard. I believe in the old saying, "Success is 97 percent perspiration and 3 percent talent." In the activity listed next, write down what you consider your main issues, challenges, or concerns regarding returning to school, and then reflect on how you can find information and support to solve these matters.

Activity: I want to learn how to deal with the following issues in order to go back to school.

What are my main concerns?	Where can I find this information?

The next two interviews in this chapter are with successful women who received education and degrees although they faced many hurdles. They believe that being a lifelong learner is a key component in today's business world. If you want the education, the next two interviews in this chapter should inspire you to go for it.

Interview with Shandra Findley

Shandra Findley is co-owner of Findley Apartments based in Las Vegas, Nevada. Her passion is to renovate apartments and to work as a substitute teacher for grades K-12 in Las Vegas. She grew up on the west side of Chicago as one of ten children.

For seventeen years, she worked for the Head Start Program in Evanston, Illinois. The purpose of the Head Start Program is to assist and educate parents on how to be more productive citizens. Through determination, hard work, and education, Shandra was able to advance at Head Start and to become co-owner of her own real estate company.

In the early 1990s, Shandra had been married and was a mother of six children living in Evanston, IL. In 1990, at the age of 36, she returned to college to get a baccalaureate degree with a major in business management from National-Louis University during a time in her life when her family was undergoing many challenges. She already had earned two associates degrees from Oakton Community College: one in early childhood education and one in marketing management. Before she returned to college, Shandra regularly took continuing education and professional development courses, and attended workshops, conferences, and seminars. She was also a well-known speaker on the educational circuit in Chicago. She believes that it is important for people to continually learn in order to reach their full potential.

Q: Was education always important to you?

FINDLEY: "Yes. As a child, both my parents and my grand-mother had stressed two things to their children when we were growing up:

1. The importance of getting an education.
2. The value of owning property.

When I was growing up, my mother was a homemaker and my father was a mechanic. My parents also owned the building where we lived. It contained our apartment as well as other apartments that my parents rented out to tenants. At the time I returned to college, my sisters and brothers had not yet completed college. I was the first one of my family of black, Catholic children raised on the west side of Chicago to receive a college degree. Most Blacks in the area at that time could not afford college; college education was considered for children of affluent families only."

Q: Did you take continuing education and professional development courses often in your career?

FINDLEY: "Absolutely. Today, you cannot get any place without an education. I worked in a field in which many women and men had already received their master's and doctorate degrees, and they believed that an education was necessary to develop the skills to succeed. The purpose of the Head Start Program was to assist and educate parents on how to be more productive citizens. By taking courses, workshops, and seminars, I had been able to work my way up into several positions at Head Start. I had gone from being a parent, to a substitute aid, to a substitute teacher, to a social service provider, and to a teacher. I chose to take non-mandatory credits in a professional development program. It was called 'Working Effectively with Difficult Family Case Studies,' and was offered at the School of Social Service Administration at the University of Chicago."

Q: Why did you go?

FINDLEY: "Because at that time I was a social worker, and I had not had any classes that dealt with difficult case studies similar to what I was handling in the Head Start Program. At all times, I really needed to know how to conduct myself in a professional manner."

Q: What is the biggest obstacle you faced to acquire an education?

FINDLEY: "Fear is a silent killer. It stops you from achieving what you could achieve, but I knew that I just had to walk through that fear and do it anyway. Growing up, my father could not write his name, but through education and with the help of his children, he learned how to not only write his name, but was able to go back to school and graduate from mechanics class at the top of his class. You have to want an education badly. I always used to say, 'Think, get in the door, start low, and watch yourself go.'"

Lessons Learned

Q: What did you learn?

FINDLEY: "I learned through valuable case studies that there is no case that is too big to handle. The courses taught me skills and gave me self-esteem, self-gratification, and the power of knowing that I could implement the skills that I had learned. Additionally, I became well-known and recognized throughout the community."

Q: How did the skills you learned transfer to your job?

FINDLEY: "My education gave me insight into what the law states, how much power I had as a social worker, what parental rights I had, and how to implement my job and enhance my abilities. It gave me a boost in my confidence to be able to handle cases in my job. Before I took the course, I questioned myself because I felt that I had not been professionally trained. I asked myself continually, 'What should you have done differently?' Once I became professionally trained, I began to believe in myself and I obtained the tools and skills needed to do a better job:

- My cases became lighter, because I knew how to handle them quickly and more efficiently.

- I was more effective in all areas of my job.

- I gained confidence in my ability.

- It raised my self-esteem.

- It gave me recognition with parents, peers, and community members.

I believe that anything that enhances one's performance or abilities is worth seeking. Additionally, you should seek it out for your own self-gratification."

Q: In 1990, you returned to get your B.A. degree at a very difficult time for you and your family. Tell me what was going on with your family.

FINDLEY: "I went back for my B.A. in business management from National-Louis University in Evanston, Illinois, at a very difficult time in my life. I was raising my six children with my husband, working as teacher in the Head Start Program, and dealing with a father who had been critically ill."

Q: With all that was going on in your life, why did you choose to return for your college degree?

FINDLEY: "I was determined to get my B.A. degree for three reasons: First, I wanted to earn more money to take care of my six children. Everyone should know that education elevates the mind and increases the income.

Secondly, I wanted to be a 'role model' to my children and the children and families in the Head Start Program, and the people in the community. My job at Head Start was to encourage low-income families to go back to school, become educated, get a trade, and get off welfare. I had to 'lead by example.' I wanted to show my children how important education was in life and that it needed to be valued.

Third, in the Head Start Program, everyone was expected to have a degree. I was in the educational field, but I didn't have the credentials expected of people in my line of work. So I felt inept. The Head Start Program was designed not only to enhance the abilities of young minds, but also to assist families in getting a higher level of education. I had always enjoyed school, and at the time I returned to school I was entering the real estate field. In business, all men that I met disregarded what I said. I figured that I would gain the knowledge and validation that I needed to be successful in business and education. Education validates your ideas in the eyes of colleagues."

Q: How was completing a college degree difficult for you in relationship to your other education programs?

FINDLEY: "It was extremely difficult to manage my time, family, work, and school. It was very demanding. It takes much longer to complete a degree than workshops or courses. I had to really be focused and want it badly. I designed a saying to tell everyone that I was getting a 'DD' degree—death or diploma, whichever one came first. That is how determined I was to complete my degree."

Q: What did earning your baccalaureate degree give you?

FINDLEY: "I improved many skills in going for my B.A. degree. I had to balance my family, work, and school. It was never easy. I:

- Learned time management skills
- Developed study techniques
- Improved my reading skills
- Learned how to take tests
- Developed writing skills.

In addition, receiving my degree has opened doors for me and given me the validation that I needed as a woman in the business world. Receiving the degree helped me to open my own business with my husband. We have Findley Apartments based in Nevada. And in turn, it has allowed me to earn more money so that I can take time off to be with my family. College is not always necessary in fields such as real estate to earn a great deal of money, but you need the education under your belt to feel confident. Knowledge is a means to enhance your own abilities to their greatest heights. I believe that a college education allowed me to develop the knowledge, skills, and the self-esteem I needed to work for myself. Also, I made some good friends in the program that I am still close to today. Since that time, I have mentored other students to help them get their college degrees. I think that one of the most important things you can do in life is to be a mentor. It means a lot to me to be able to share what I've learned—about education and about life itself—with other people."

Interview with Nancy Suvarnamani
Benefits of Advanced Degrees and
Designations in the Field

After earning two master's degrees, Nancy Suvarnamani sought advanced designations in her field. She believes this is a wonderful way to gain credibility, knowledge, skills, and tools, as well as form friendships, network, and build relationships in a field.

Biography

Nancy Suvarnamani is president and broker/owner of Century 21 SGR Inc., which has three offices in Chicago, one in Lakeview, one in South Loop, and one in West Loop. She has a staff of over eighty sales agents, and she will be the next president of the Chicago Association of REALTORS®. She has more than eighteen years' experience in the real estate industry and has been the broker/owner of Century 21 SGR, Inc. since 1989. She has received honors as the leading sales associate in the Century 21 Metropolitan Chicago Region. She is also one of the leading marketers of new developments in the Chicagoland Area, and she has been a top producer for Century 21.

Nancy is a firm believer that education adds value to you. She has received many degrees and designations, and she continues to take programs offered in her field. Her credentials include:

- B.A. degree in political science, Chiengmai University, Thailand
- Master's in social science, Northeastern Illinois University
- Master's in information science, Northern Illinois University
- Century 21 International, Management Training
- Century 21 ORBIT Advance Management Training
- Century 21 Commercial Investment Network (CIN)
- NAR's Certified International Property Specialist (CIPS)
- NAR's Council of Real Estate Brokerage Managers (CRB).

In addition, she maintains membership and is active in several professional associations:

- Chicago Association of REALTORS® (CAR), president-elect of CAR

- Illinois Association of Realtors (IAR)

- National Association of Women Business Owners (NAWBO).

Take Advanced Degrees in Your Field

Q: How and why did you take the advanced degrees?

SUVARNAMANI: "I had come to the United States from Thailand to take a master's of science degree. I wanted to get an education to teach information technology and science in a university. I had a dream of becoming a professor even though I knew that professors did not make a great deal of money. At the time, I was working for Beatrice Foods, and I had earned a scholarship to take the master's degree."

Q: How did you get started in the real estate business?

SUVARNAMANI: "I was enrolled in the master's program, and I started working part-time in real estate. I learned almost immediately that in the real estate field there are unlimited possibilities to make money. The business is like going fishing in the ocean; you can fish all night in the ocean, because there are unlimited fish to catch. I also learned that regardless of your culture, sex, age, or language, if you work hard the possibilities to make money and do a great service for people are unlimited. So I began working in the real estate business full-time."

Learn to Deal with Obstacles

Q: What were the obstacles that you had to overcome to receive these degrees?

SUVARNAMANI: "I was working full-time. Therefore, I had to attend class at night and on weekends. I was always very tired, but I was determined to receive my degrees. I had to stay focused and plan every day how I could do all the work. I would write out my 'to-do list' each morning, and I would focus on staying on track each week. I would write my assignments out by hand and then type them later."

Q: Why did you go back for your CIPS (Certified International Property Specialist) designation?

SUVARNAMANI: "I had learned a great deal about technology in my other educational programs, but I wanted to do international business transactions, and I needed to learn how. The Certified International Property Specialist (CIPS) degree taught me the skills, knowledge, and tools that I needed to do international business deals."

Q: What did the advanced designation in your field provide for your career?

SUVARNAMANI: "I learned how to do international transactions, and I gained credibility that distinguishes me in my field. My other degrees taught me about political science and technology, but before taking the CIPS, I had not learned anything about doing business internationally. I now belong to a network that contains many people in my country. Even though new technology is much cheaper today and I can use my cell phone to call anywhere in the world, I learned that I still have to go to my home country to do business. Real estate is a business in which the people in Asian countries still want to see you in person and get to know you. It is a relationship business where people have to see you face-to-face, get to know you, and trust you in order to do business."

Q: What were the obstacles that you had to overcome to receive these degrees and how were they different from when you were in school for your master's degrees?

SUVARNAMANI: "At the time, I was very tired, and I had a very heavy schedule. However, I knew from the experience of taking the other programs how to plan to complete this one. I continued to write a to-do list every morning, and during the week I would set aside time to complete the homework. However, now I have a typist/assistant to type my material. But, my time is even more limited because I own a real estate company that employs more than eighty people in three locations. My business is continually growing. So I have to really budget my time, plan carefully, and stay focused."

Q: How are you capitalizing on your education?

SUVARNAMANI: "I am currently doing international business deals. With new technological advances, our countries are globally linked, and it is much easier to do international business deals. The advanced designations have opened my eyes to the international marketplace. I am currently doing business with people in Thailand who are investing in commercial properties in the United States. There are many places in the world where people want to bring money and invest in businesses in the United States."

Advice on Success from Nancy

Q: What advice do you have for others seeking education to advance in their career?

SUVARNAMANI: "I would suggest that people join professional associations and get involved and further their education in their field. I am the past vice chairman of the International Real Estate Committee and current president-elect for the Chicago Association of REALTORS®, and I am a member of the Federation of International Real Estate Professionals (FIABCI). In America, the opportunities to make money are endless for anyone who wants to work hard and learn. I would love for other women and minorities to realize that there are scholarships available in the United States to pay for college programs. Education is important for everyone today in business."

Author's Concluding Tips

Both women persevered through their fears, their obstacles, and their challenges in their personal and professional lives to obtain education and credentials in their fields. Although they acknowledge that pursuing education or training programs was often very difficult for them, they believe, as I do, that you need to obtain at all costs what is required in your field to be successful. As in the words of Shandra Findley, "I made up my mind I was going for a 'DD' Degree—Death or Diploma, which ever came first." Hopefully, after reading their stories, you are ready to examine your fears and your issues and pursue the education required to be successful in your field.

Step 5: Start a Career Plan

Interview with Patricia Choi

"ENJOY THE JOURNEY"

7. Work Hard and Leverage Each Job to Create Your Perfect Career!

6. Put Plan into Action

5. Start a Career Plan

4. Educate Yourself

3. Learn About the Field

2. Examine Your Talents

1. Organize

Drawing by Phil Orlandi

Chapter Five

Step 5: Start a Career Plan

"Know what your niche is, and be the best at it."

—Patricia Choi

Points to Remember

➤ Develop a career/business plan.

➤ Set career goals and objectives.

➤ Write your mission statement/philosophy.

➤ Maintain your office equipment.

➤ Keep separate email addresses.

➤ Consider Web site development and other marketing ideas.

➤ Get business cards.

➤ Create a marketing plan.

➤ Create a career action plan.

➤ Keep portfolio ready and "career central."

At one time in their careers, all of the interviewees in this book, whether they wanted to open a business or simply get a job in an organization, sat down and designed a detailed career plan. This chapter guides you on the basic information and skills you need to know to design your plan. For example, Patricia Choi, the subject of this chapter, sat down with her husband and colleagues and designed a business plan before opening CHOI International. After David Leeds wrote a plan for his career future, he realized that he not only wanted to move into a senior leadership position at Allstate, but he also wanted to use his talents, education, and connections to become a professor of adult education upon his retirement. Also, Ruth Theobald has built onto her successful business as a trainer/consultant to add new aspects to her career as an author and motivational speaker.

So what are you waiting for? Start it now! If nothing else, writing this plan will help you clarify your goals, develop your mission and philosophy, see how much money it will take, and open your eyes to see new opportunities. To get the overall picture, there are many basic subjects that you need to be familiar with—they are too detailed to present here. For more information, go to the Web or to your local bookstore.

Set Career Goals and Objectives

1. Description of business type, vision, philosophy, niche, purpose: what, where, why, and how of the business
2. Financial strategy or budget:
   A. List of expected costs and expenses that will include: supplies and e-commerce costs, such as Web site design, development, and maintenance

B. Business equipment including all office, phone, computer, paper, pens

C. Marketing and advertising expenses, such as fliers, brochures, business cards, and résumés, cost of balancing books, taxes, insurance

3. Explanation of where, how, and when you will get the money

4. List of required license, education, and work experience

5. Explanation of your targeted market

6. Statement regarding when/how you will reach your goals.

Write Your Mission Statement or Philosophy

Every person should have a written mission and/or philosophy statement. This document should be about one page in length. It should explain your personal beliefs and values and how you would practice them in a work setting. If you want to be the best at something, then you must not only decide what that means, you should also be able to articulate it to other people. Even if you do not plan to show this document to a potential employer, you need to write it *as if* you're planning to do so. An effective mission statement must at least:

1. Describe your purpose

2. Describe your personal career philosophy—what you believe in or stand for

3. List the principles, beliefs, or values that will guide your work

4. Explain how you are going to address these values in your work.

Begin the process of filling out the next activity sheet based on your answers to these four questions. List any words, phrases, or ideas that first come into your head with respect to these various categories. Do not edit at this point. Look for language and concepts that will enjoy broad acceptance in your field, but make sure that they reflect your true beliefs. Do not write what you think people want to hear, but instead write what you value, what you bring to your work, and how you believe you will practice it. People will know if your statement is insincere, and that will hurt you in the long run.

If you plan to show this philosophy statement to get work or to help you, then you should continue to develop it, but do not worry about that now. More importantly, just put it down on paper.

Activity: My Personal Philosophy Is:

1. I believe that I stand for _____

_____

2. My purpose is _____

_____

3. The principles, beliefs, or values that will guide my work are

_____

4. I am going to address these values in my work by _____

_____

_____

_____

In addition, if you are opening your own business, I suggest that you take this same format and write another one-page mission statement for your organization.

Activity: My Mission or Philosophy for My Organization. What My Organization Stands For.

_____

_____

_____

_____

_____

_____

_____

_____

_____

_____

_____

_____

Maintain Your Office Equipment

Keep your information and business equipment updated and available. This area should preferably be some place other than your office in case you have to leave your current company in a hurry. In real estate, most brokers and sales people, regardless of whether they work for a large or small company, have a home office. In addition, they usually store much of their information on portable computers, cell phones, etc. so that they can conduct business anywhere in the world. Today, with rapid changes in business, I think this is a great idea regardless of what field or what organization you work for. Who knows? Maybe you will have a sick day, and you can still complete your work assignment on time if you have access to the information you need.

I recommend that everyone should always be ready to market him or herself at a moment's notice. Whether you plan to stay with one company, move to other organizations, or open your own business, you should set up an area in your home as a duplicate office, complete with the following items:

- Computer
- Printer/copier
- Phone
- Fax
- Paper
- Pens, pencils.

Keep Separate Email Addresses

It is always a good idea to keep a separate email address for professional career development, especially if you work in a firm where your records are kept on their machines. In a case where the organization goes out of business or is consolidated, or if in the worst case you are let go, you need to have all your personal career records immediately accessible. (Do not confuse that information with the organization's business documents; I am not telling you to keep their records, but instead, I am encouraging you to keep building your own portfolio of education, credentials, awards, speaking engagements, etc.) You want to always build your career in a professional manner—like a house built on a solid foundation, a well-constructed career will not collapse.

Get Business Cards

Even if you are not opening your own business, it is a great idea for you to have business cards. Of course, if you are planning to open a business, then business cards, fliers, and a Web site are absolute necessities. There are reputable sites on the Web where you can get business cards printed inexpensively or sometimes even free; check Vistacards.com or other similar Web sites.

It will always help your career if you write and speak on what you know, and you can use these business tools to get new speaking and writing positions.

Consider Web Site Development and Other Marketing Ideas

Having a Web site is a terrific way to draw people to you (the ones you want). With the wonders of new technology, you can design your own Web site if you possess the skills, and have the energy and the time. But I would suggest for your first time, since it needs to look professional, you should hire a professional. In my opinion, it is money well spent.

Whether you or someone else is designing it, look at people's Web sites who do what you do, but please don't copy them—that is unlawful. Just use them to get some ideas of what you like and do not like. Then, write your ideas on paper. If someone else is designing your Web site, be sure to have him or her incorporate your ideas into it so that it truly advertises the best of you.

My personal recommendations about Web sites:

- Content should be the most important aspect, not pictures etc.

- Make sure it is designed to relate to your audience

- Have site reviewed by other colleagues and professionals

- Make it very easy for people to contact you

- Design Web site so you can advertise your services, products, articles, etc.

- Promote your Web site on everything you do: business cards, letters, speaking engagements, etc.

Several sites that you can look at
offer templates for your Web site
to help you:

www.bigstep.com
www.bcentral.com
www.yahoo.com

If you still want to do this on your own, go to bookstores, libraries, or online to learn what is involved.

If you are trying to get the word out about what you want, it is
great to have all of the above to market yourself. Business cards, fliers, and brochures can really promote your business and give you
a brand. Think of a slogan for your business cards and fliers that
answers the question, "Why should I hire you?" or "What makes you
different from everyone else?" A catchy phrase or slogan ensures
people will ALWAYS associate you or your company name with their
product or services. People remember great TV ads even after the
commercial is over. It is called *branding*. Companies pay big bucks to
advertising agencies to come up with these lasting slogans. Consider
doing the exact same thing on marketing materials. You want people
to remember you after you meet. You can design these items and

print them yourself at home, or hire a professional through the Web, referrals, or at a store like Kinko's in your area. These marketing tools can help you tremendously. Three important tips to remember are:

1. Never leave home without your business card. Have them with your wallet/money, house keys, and driver's license. Any "per chance" meeting is an opportunity to give out a business card.

2. Give business cards out to everyone, including family and friends, at job fairs, conferences, etc.

3. Insert a business card when mailing bill payments.

Create a Marketing Plan

Now, regardless of whether you are building your career by owning your own business or working in an organization, you need to develop a marketing plan for serving your clients. Many successful people who become leaders, CEOs, or chairmen of companies run the organization as if they were entrepreneurs. All the people I have interviewed believe so much in their work that they act as if the business is their own and try to constantly think of new ways for adding value to themselves, their workplaces, and the world. In my opinion, to maintain an acceptable level of professionalism, you have to operate in such a way that you satisfy your customers by developing a better product or a better service, or both. And I believe a very important part of success is to know who your clients are and how to serve them, whether you serve them personally or not. The best way to do that is to complete the next activity.

CHOI: "I was born and raised in Birmingham, Alabama. I had worked as a paralegal for almost twenty years, and for personal and professional reasons, I needed a major change in my life. So I moved from Birmingham to Honolulu, Hawaii, in 1975 to be a paralegal with the law firm of Torkildson, Katz, Conahan, & Loden. The firm specialized in tax and real estate. I met my husband, Cedric Choi, who was an associate attorney at the firm."

Q: How did you enter into the real estate business?

CHOI: "After a short time, the law firm I was with decided to open a real estate company to represent their wealthy clients, and they asked me if I would like to head the real estate company. I was delighted to learn something new; I always loved learning. As head of their company, I represented their clients for almost four years— and immediately, I loved the real estate business and the clientele."

Q: Why did you open your own business?

CHOI: "As soon as I became involved in the real estate field, I realized that this was a field I was born to be in. So I discussed how much I loved the business with my husband, and in 1981, I started my own 'boutique' real estate firm, specializing in luxury real estate and commercial properties. Over the last twenty-three years, I have been involved in real estate sales, and I have been very happy. This is my perfect career field. I saw it as a great opportunity. I realized immediately that I could not beat that I was 'in the right place at the right time' to have the right opportunity, and my skills were perfect for the field."

Q: Did you have a mentor who helped you find your talents and the right opportunities for you in opening your business?

CHOI: "Yes, I think a mentor is very important. My mentor was Elliot H. Loden, a tax lawyer at Torkildson Law Firm, and he was my inspiration and most instrumental in my career change into real estate. He taught me a lot about taxes and real estate and made sure that I got the right opportunities and clients. Nobody is self-made in the sense that they don't have someone who mentors/teaches them; you always need to build relationships."

Q: What skills and strategies did you use to start your successful business plan?

CHOI: "Other than being in the right place at the right time and having the right talents, I would say there were several factors that I defined first to opening my business:

- I recognized a need or 'niche' for the business.

- I was passionate about it—I loved the business.

- I had experience working in the field for several years.

- I knew what market I would pursue.

- I knew who my customers were.

- I had built great connections.

- I had an education and license in the field.

- I knew where/how to learn vital information.

- I had professionals who were willing to help.

I picked a great partner who balances my skills, my husband, Cedric Choi. Cedric is vice president and managing director of CHOI International. He manages the staff and agents totaling more than thirty people. Cedric has been a practicing attorney for twenty-five years. He is a graduate of Punahou School, Stanford, and the University of Santa Clara School of Law. Cedric also has recognition in the field from his writing; he co-authored *The Complete Guide to Preventing and Resolving Brokerage Disputes for Investors, Advisors and Attorneys*. In addition, we decided early on to hire only trained, seasoned agents, as well as licensed assistants. You must set up a business with the right people."

Q: Did you decide from the start to build a market niche business?

CHOI: "Yes, from the inception, we had a vision of building a niche. The firm's motto is: 'Extraordinary properties, unrivaled expertise.' We help the wealthy buyer or seller with the best professional service possible. We are a 'boutique' Hawaii real-estate brokerage company with the exclusive right to sell many of Hawaii's finest residential and select commercial properties. We are known for providing the best service, expertise, and professionalism in the area. We provide our clients with every possible service and amenity. We are the best at what we do. People come to Hawaii for the fresh air, pure water, and weather. Many people make purchases more for emotional and personal reasons than purely financial reasons—and many pay in cash. So mortgages and interest rate fluctuations have little impact on their decisions. Instead, people make the difference. We very much have a concierge or boutique service, providing whatever the clients need including understanding their culture, language, how to do financial transactions between countries, etc. We have agents who speak different languages, which is very important. We cover Japanese, Taiwanese, Mandarin, Korean, English, Spanish, French, and Italian."

Q: What type of education have you received? And has it helped you in your business?

CHOI: "My education has been very influential in my success. I am a licensed broker. I have achieved the coveted designation as a CCIM (Certified Commercial Investment Member), held by fewer than 15,000 of the 1,000,000 realtors in the nation and the international real estate designation of CIPS (Certified International Property Specialist), as well as being a founding member of the Institute for Certified Luxury Home Specialists. Real estate professionals can earn designations and degrees in real estate, and it really gives you recognition and the tools you need to do international business. I believe the CCIM was like getting a college education, and few women in the field have received it."

Lessons Learned

Q: What other factors do you think you needed to start your business in what you feel is your perfect career, and do you feel these same skills are necessary if you want to become a leader within an organization?

CHOI: "Yes, absolutely. There were several key factors that helped me succeed in starting and building my business career that would be right for others who want to develop their career potential, whether it's as a leader within an organization or to build their own business in many fields. For instance:

1. *I Am Very Entrepreneurial.* From the start, I built a sound business plan with an outstanding partner and staff, had the finances

arranged, and set up an office using the best technology. These factors helped us to start in a strong position for success. If you look at many real estate people, as in other careers, even if they hold their license and work for a real estate company, they must act like entrepreneurs in order to be successful.

2. *I Wanted to Provide Top Customer Service.* We are a concierge service. Whatever our customer wants, we take care of that in every way possible. I consider myself a perfectionist. I pay extra attention to detail. This trait suits my profession well because our clients demand close attention to detail, and expect customer service somewhere close to perfection. But at the same time, I am very flexible in order to be able to meet the clients' needs. When you call my office for me, a receptionist takes down all the information and gives it to me. I do not want clients to get recorded messages when they call. I feel that customer service is important in most careers. Often, I think many people fail because they do not know who their customers are or their needs in the field. I also had great past experiences in the business to draw from when designing my business, but I make sure we keep abreast of the knowledge of the market and any new developments in the industry.

3. *I Had Built Relationships.* I have built great networks and personal relationships with people I deal with so that I can pick

up the phone and call them. I understand the buyers, their personalities, and lifestyles. I like people and I cultivate personal relationships.

4. *I Value Being Professional.* We service our clients with integrity, honesty, and a commitment to excellence. We have built a great reputation. Part of our job is to help homebuyers understand the value of the home they are looking at given that luxury homes are in limited supply here. I also wanted to build trust by being very discreet. You have to know what your business requires, but we really offer concierge services with quiet confidentiality. Movie stars, producers, and celebrities have purchased some of the homes, and I am strict about their confidentiality. Discretion is the absolute rule for any REALTOR® serving this class of clientele. After a while, many of my clients want to come to Oahu for its cultures, arts, and access to airports and medical facilities, and they also want to feel like 'kamaaina'—becoming a real part of the community. We are proud of this—fostering trust is as important as experience, knowledge, and a connection to the luxury-home community and you have to manage that carefully.

5. *I Have a Great Work Ethic.* I work hard seven days a week and do an exceptional job, meeting with clients when it's most convenient for them. I am also selective about the properties I represent. When our sign goes up in front, it's usually a property of high-quality distinction.

6. *I Have Patience.* While the mantra for most REALTORS® would be 'location, location, location,' I believe in my business it is also timing, perseverance, and patience. It can take anywhere from two weeks to five years for potential buyers to make up their minds. Many of the buyers have several homes around the globe, and they pass through Hawaii during their world gallops. So patience is important to selling. I have steely patience beneath a professional exterior.

7. *I Am Very Persistent.* From the very beginning in selling real estate, I have been called, 'a saleswoman who's really persistent, and who always looks for a new angle to sell.' I have sold one house five times—the first time for $700,000 in 1978 and the fifth time for $1.6 million in 1990. Another Kahala oceanfront property sold for $2.6 million in 1986 and $9 million in 2003. Often, when a client feels that he has missed an opportunity to purchase a home, he may return a year later and offer up to $1 million more than the original asking price. The average turnaround for buying and selling homes is about five to ten years. Then luxury homeowners often want to try out another part of the globe before returning to buy in our area, but I keep ties to them for future sales. As is true in many fields, you must be willing to sell your ideas.

8. *I Have Built a Team of Professionals.* Selling a luxury home means dealing with a team of professionals rather than just one individual—ranging from financial advisers, to attorneys, to house-

keepers, to managers. The key is to become the spoke in the wheel in managing all of the different team players. It is also about creating good relationships with clients. To make the transactions smoother, CHOI International also provides asset management, including legal and tax coordination services and referrals to housekeeping and maintenance. As I mentioned earlier, the real estate team hires people to speak Japanese, Mandarin, German, Taiwanese, English, Korean, Spanish, French, and Italian to serve an international clientele.

9. *I Began Getting Involved in My Community.* I have distinguished myself as a leader in regional, national, and international real estate organizations by being well connected to my community's activities. Locally, I was the first recipient of the Aloha Aina Real Estate Award as the Realtor's Choice in 1998 for my service to the industry and clients, my professional and ethical conduct, my cooperative business approaches, and extraordinary service to all in transactions. I was appointed by the governor to the Real Estate Commission of the State of Hawaii, to which I devote part of my time to public service. I am very active as a director and volunteer fund-raiser for various charitable institutions, such as the YMCA and for the restoration of Washington Place (Governor's Mansion). All these connections have helped me build my business, and at the same time, give back to the community and the field that has been so good to me.

10. *I Am Very Active in Real Estate Associations and Organizations.* I serve in leadership roles. This helps me learn new information, network, and build relationships—that's key to success in any field. I have been active in the National Association of Realtors International Operations Committee and received an award as the Outstanding International Reciprocal Director to Korea for 2000. I really keep involved with arenas that are unique to my business. I believe that my involvement in the international arena has led to my selection as an affiliate of LuxuryRealEstate.com, an exclusive organization of five hundred of the world's top brokers. LuxuryRealEstate.com has been recognized as having the favorite luxury real estate site by *Forbes Magazine.* The organization is made up of the best luxury brokerage houses in each region and represents twenty-five countries with over $3 billion of luxury real estate. Membership is by invitation only."

Q: Do you have some tips on marketing your business?

CHOI: "Absolutely. Technology has really been a blessing to us. We created a top Web site. Our Web site was a model for the Honolulu Board of REALTORS®. In addition to personal referrals, many potential homebuyers find their information on the Web. The CHOI International Web site, www.CHOI-realty.com, has been a good way to reach out to potential homebuyers worldwide. My firm is the leader in luxury real estate Internet marketing.

"I believe in the saying, 'You are often judged by the company you keep.' And I have a membership in 'Who's Who in Luxury Real Estate,' an international network informing potential clients about like-minded brokers and their listings worldwide. This was started about fifteen years ago by Seattle-based broker John Brian Losh. 'Who's Who' has grown from a modest company of 150 select brokers interested in networking and sharing potential leads into one that today includes five hundred members in twenty-five countries. The only way to become a member is at the personal invitation of Losh, who travels the world to meet with and select brokers based on referrals, listings, and testimony from clients. Typically, members are boutique firms specializing in luxury. This is a wonderful way to network and market my business."

Advice on Success from Patricia

Q: Do you have any other advice you would like to offer?

CHOI: "If you find your perfect field, like I did, seize the opportunity to build your career. Plan it, develop it, work hard, and be professional. Reputation is important, but also very important, as in many careers, you cannot succeed if you do not provide outstanding customer service tailored to your clients' needs. You must define who your clients are in your career. Are you working face-to-face or by telephone or email? You must know the protocol for working with your particular population. We work with people from different countries whose first language is often not English. We have to become experts in their culture, their customs, their ways of doing business, and we have people who understand their language, even the protocol for using telephones, faxes, letters, etc. The success of CHOI International is attributed to our custom-tailored service to meet the needs of our individual clients as well as the very talented and professional staff with more than twenty-five years of Hawaii real estate experience.

"Try to find a mentor as I did. Nobody is self-made in the sense that they have to have someone who mentors or teaches them; you always need to build relationships.

"Whatever field you choose, you should continue to learn. One area that I found is changing rapidly is technology. Today, you can market your business by using Web sites, but do not forget the personal relationships. When someone calls our company, they get a person, not a machine, who is well trained on professional service. Nothing, in my opinion, will replace personal customer service.

"I also would suggest becoming involved in your community and professional organizations. Start out spending time and not worrying about what you get back. It will enhance your personal satisfaction, and eventually also your business relationships. People know if you are genuine. But again the most important advice I can give you is, know what your niche is, and be the best at it."

Author's Concluding Tips

Patricia Choi's career really took off once she found her field, developed her niche, and decided to open her own business. In short, she followed the old saying, "Put your money where your mouth is," and certainly once you have found your talents, you need to commit your time, energy, focus, and most importantly, write a formal career plan to move forward in your career. The next chapter will tell you steps to do so immediately.

Step 6: Put Your Plan into Action

Interview with Steven L. Good

"ENJOY THE JOURNEY"

7. Work Hard and Leverage Each Job to Create Your Perfect Career!

6. Put Plan into Action

5. Start a Career Plan

4. Educate Yourself

3. Learn About the Field

2. Examine Your Talents

1. Organize

*Drawing by
Phil Orlandi*

Chapter Six

Step 6: Put Your Plan into Action

"Challenge yourself to go after what you want, and have fun while you are doing it."
—Steven L. Good

Points to Remember

➤ Network, network, and network—with friends, family, business people.

➤ Join professional organizations and serve in leadership roles.

➤ Do internships.

➤ Speak on what you know.

➤ Mentor others.

➤ Teach/train others.

➤ Write and publish in your field.

➤ Continue to learn and research your field.

➤ Continue to develop your résumé.

➤ Keep letters of recommendation.

➤ Continue to send out your résumé.

There are many ways to go after your dream career. This chapter discusses some tips for putting your plan into action immediately. Whether your dream career is working for an organization or owning your own business, you must follow your dream career regardless of your age. There is a book I referred to earlier titled *Feel the Fear and Do It Anyway*. I believe that nothing that is "safe" is as exciting as the feeling of accomplishment that follows doing something you feared. Remember the proverb, "Actions speak louder than words." I believe firmly that if you want to reach your career goals, at some point, you must decide to put action steps into your daily routine. The next section provides an overview of some actions you can take right now to pursue your career. Once you take the leap, I think you will find that what you mistook for fear is really the exhilarating thrill of breaking out of your old daily grind to take a chance on something meaningful and deeply rewarding.

Although you have used many of these strategies in the earlier steps, before you were networking, joining organizations, doing internships, etc. as "research" into a field. Now you've committed to the field and are doing the strategies as a way to find the perfect job and further your career. You may be doing the same things but you're doing them for a different reason.

Network, Network, and Network

One way to get what you want is to network with as many people as you know. You can start by talking about your career goals with your family and friends. They will have many suggestions for you—both good and bad. Take the suggestions and use the information to move forward in a positive manner. People closest to you may not share your visions, but they will almost certainly provide support and connections to help you move forward. All you need to do is ask.

Join Professional Organizations and Serve in Leadership Roles

Join professional organizations in your field, and once you have joined, offer to work on committees and find ways to serve in leadership roles. This is a great way to learn more about your chosen field from the inside, and nine times out of ten, organizations are desperate for people who have the time and the willingness to do the work. Be one of these rare individuals and your efforts will pay off. If you are not familiar with organizations in your area, I suggest you go on the Internet and find recognized professional associations in your field. Be sure to check out the organization to make sure it is credible before you join. Volunteer work can provide many opportunities for you:

- Learn about your career
- Get valuable experience
- Add value to the organization
- Network and build relationships in your field
- Make friendships.

Do Internships

Doing internships is another terrific way to learn about your field. Often, when you take college programs, they will offer you an internship in order to complete a degree. For instance, Roosevelt University's MBA in real estate program offers internships as part of the curriculum. I believe that if you can get an internship through any organization or school, it is a wonderful way to learn about your field. You should take the initiative to approach companies and ask them to give you an internship. Jack Canfield writes in *Make College Easier: Fire Up Your Dreams and Get a Very Cool Job, 4th Edition*: "According to a 1997 study at Northwestern University 64 percent of interns are eventually offered jobs with their host employees" (p. 109). If you can, consider working a second shift in your field on weekends or evenings. This is a great way to gain credentials and experience you can use in your field.

Speak on What You Know

I believe that speaking on what you know is a way for you to continue to learn on your subject, teach others, and build your business. Whatever your expertise may be, consider speaking at meetings of appropriate organizations. There are many ways to begin: Either volunteer to speak at organizations where you are connected or explore the Web or telephone book for organizations that would be interested in your topic. Then put together a list of organizations that you would like to talk to; start in the yellow pages under "service organizations." Once you have decided on an organization, write a nice cover letter introducing yourself and give a brief overview of your presentation need. Send out twenty letters on your personal letterhead. If you have a personal brochure, of course include it with the letter. The people who do this tell me that after the first three or four presentations, you will feel totally relaxed and find you no longer have any fear about speaking in public. Build a niche that is unique to you. By doing this, you can produce a steady flow of two or three speaking opportunities every month.

Teach/Train Others

I believe that through teaching others either through a course, in groups, or one-on-one, you not only provide a valuable service, but you also learn in the process. As I express on my Web site, www.drmargotweinstein.com, I believe in the words by Albert Einstein, "Setting an example is not the main means of influencing others, it is the only means." My prescription for happiness as listed on my Web site is: "First, find your passion by examining stories of successful people. Then, work hard to perfect your talents while enjoying your journey. And last, teach your journey to help others find their way." For the past two years, I have been working with students at Inter-American Magnet School in Chicago to teach children about writing, homeownership, and careers in real estate. I have learned a great deal from the students and teachers from the experience.

Mentor Others

I believe that being a role model to others is valuable to everyone involved. You will learn, provide help to someone else, and probably find new connections from the relationship.

Write and Publish in Your Field

Writing can help you clarify your goals, gain new insight, and gain credibility and recognition. Today, with all the online publications and new technologies, there are so many more ways to publish your work than there were a few years ago. You can offer to write about your career in a community newspaper, through your professional organization, or through self-publications.

Continue to Learn and Research Your Field

I have learned by conducting interviews with very successful people that they always value lifelong learning to build their careers. You will see that is a common thread that binds together all the interviews in this book. You should always be open to learning new ideas. Another great way to learn is by using the Internet to find information about your career. Others are:

- Libraries

- Bookstores

- Seminars, conferences, and workshops.

Continue to Develop Your Résumé

Continue to update your résumé with new positions, speaking engagements, publications, volunteer activities, etc. You never know when you will need to send it to someone, so keeping it up to date will prevent lots of midnight-hour scrambling to try to pull all your information together and write it up. (If you're not naturally organized, you probably know this unpleasant feeling well!)

Keep Letters of Recommendation

It is also valuable in most fields to show people examples of current successful performance. My daughter taught me to keep three letters of recommendation handy to give people when going on job interviews. She uses them to give out to acquire part-time work.

Continue to Send out Your Résumé

You can carry résumés with you to hand out in person. You can also send résumés through fax, email, and mail, but first check on the "do not call laws" in the state. You may have to have had some previous introduction to the organization, due to all the new governmental regulations. I believe that the best way to handle this is to have someone introduce you to a person in the organization before you send a résumé. Your résumés can be sent by fax, email, or mail, but always find out what the organization prefers. If they offer online submission of résumés, I suggest you send yourself a copy for your records. Sometimes email attachments look different on paper than on the screen, so I always send myself the attachment and open it, print it, and save it for my records.

More Interview Tips

- *Learn About Your Industry, Company, and Position Beforehand.* Before going to a company, do research on the company's background, focus, philosophy, mission, company personnel, and market conditions. So many people go to an interview without doing their homework. Carry résumés with you to give in person.

- *Be Persistent.* Once you have sent your résumé, be persistent, but do not be a pest—sometimes there is a fine line and you need to learn where it is drawn. Call to follow up after an interview, to set up additional interviews, or find out why you were not selected.

As you work toward finding your niche, the next activity should trigger some new avenues for you to pursue.

Activity: What I Want to Pursue to Build My Business

Activities I want to pursue:	When	Where
Do an internship		
Join a professional organization		
Speak on what I know		
Do volunteer work		
Find a mentor		
Mentor others		
Write on my career		
Develop my résumé/ vitae		
Get letters of recommendation		
Develop interview skills		

Interview with Steven L. Good

This next story is of a man who found his dream career after he entered his father's business as a part-time job in his college years. Through hard work and persistence, Steven L. Good built his father's business into the #1 firm selling real estate at auctions throughout the United States, and had fun doing it. (His father, Sheldon Good, was the head of Sheldon Good & Company and a very successful professional.) I have learned through several years of covering Steven Good that even though he was able to enter his father's business, the strategies he used to build his career and his company and the advice he offers here are essential for success. Whether you plan to reach your goals within an organization or start your own business, you can put your career plan into motion and move forward toward your dream career if you pay attention to the strategies Steven Good presents in this chapter.

Biography

Attorney **Steven L. Good** is chairman and CEO of Sheldon Good & Company. Steven has been the driving force in the recent expansion of Sheldon Good & Company, considered to be America's premier auction company specializing in using auctions to market some of the world's most unusual real estate. The company was started by

Steve's father, Sheldon Good, in 1965 and has its corporate head-quarters in Chicago, Illinois.

In the Summer of 2001, Steven Good completed the purchase of Sheldon Good & Company International and its subsidiaries from his father, Sheldon Good. Steven L. Good, at age 44, became the chairman and CEO of Sheldon Good & Company International, LLC, a newly-formed corporate partnership that was established as a result of the sale. After the partnership was formed, Sheldon Good became chairman emeritus of the new company, signed a long-term agreement to continue developing new business for the thirty-six-year-old real estate marketing and auction firm bearing his name. Sheldon Good & Company handles more than seventy different classes of real estate and has sold more than 40,000 properties and has completed over $8 billion in closed transactions since 1965.

Steven Good is a member of many professional organizations. He is the 121st president of the Chicago Association of REALTORS®, the third largest real estate professional association in the United States, and is the author of a best-selling book, *Churches, Jails, and Gold Mines ... Mega-Deals from a Real Estate Maverick*. Good is widely interviewed as an established authority in the field of high-level real estate auctions and is published in numerous publications: *The National Law Journal, Real Estate, The Chicago Sun-Times*, and *Real Estate Review*.

Steven Good earned his B.S. degree in finance (magna cum laude) from Syracuse University and a Juris Doctor from DePaul University College of Law. He is an accredited auctioneer of real estate (AARE), and he received an honorary Doctor of Humane Letters from Robert Morris College for his work with students.

Q: Before you decided that real estate was your perfect career, you had taken several other part-time jobs and internships, right?

GOOD: "Yes. I spent my sophomore year in college working for Adlai Stevenson III, who was serving as a U.S. Senator at that time. When I was admitted to the School, I was assigned to work as Tyrone Fayner's administrative assistant when he was the director of the Department of State Police. Tyrone Fayner ultimately ran Mayer, Brown, Platt & Wood, and was Attorney General. Another summer I got a job working as Tom Tully's speech writer for the Cook County Assessor's Office."

Q: How did you get your internships?

GOOD: "In my sophomore year in college, I started getting internships thanks to letters of request that I had written to many famous politicians. Later on, my connections got me several internships."

Q: What did you learn from working in other fields?

GOOD: "All through my college years and in law school, I took several jobs and internships as a way of broadening my experience and my network of friends, building my résumé, and being recognized for doing a good job. I realized early that internships were a good way of getting great experience that I otherwise would not be able to get in business. I worked for various prominent statesmen and politicians and saw how things worked in the business world, learned what I liked and didn't like, and what ethically fit my beliefs. I worked as Tom Tully's speech writer for the Cook County Assessor's Office. At that time I was interested in going to law school, but I was not sure that I wanted to practice law as a career. As an undergraduate student, I worked in the Senate, which is where they make laws. The following summer, I worked in the law enforcement area so I was able to see how they enforced the laws. Working for the Cook County Assessor's Office was invaluable because the office has everything to do with assessing real property in one of the largest communities in the country.

"From these experiences, I learned that I did not want to be a prosecutor, because of the ethical and moral dilemmas that one has in that system (i.e., a prosecutor's job is to bring someone to jail; a defense attorney's job is to get someone out of jail). I asked myself, 'What happens when you're not sure that the defendant is guilty? Or what if you're not sure the defendant is innocent?' And ultimately that whole concept ran counter to my personality. So I learned from these experiences that I did not want to become a practicing lawyer."

Q: How did you get started in the real estate business?

GOOD: "In 1980, I took a summer job working for my father at Sheldon Good & Company, and I loved the business from the beginning. I sold a big building and made a big commission, which kind of moved me toward the money side of life."

Q: After taking a summer job with your father, you found a perfect career and continue to expand your company niche from it. Do you believe that your story can provide insight to others looking to build their careers?

GOOD: "Absolutely. You should always use your education, experiences, and personal abilities to move forward. During my summer job at Sheldon Good & Company, I realized that the business was a perfect fit for me. Immediately, I decided that I liked the transactional side of the business, and I wanted to be in the brokerage business and build our auction business, which was only a small part of our company at that time. Because of my educational and business background, I thought that auctions made a lot of sense for many different reasons:

"First, the auction business was in its infancy, and our company had the luxury of not having a strong competitor.

"In addition, there was a great negativity about people doing auctions for real estate properties at that time. As a result, most people in the brokerage business did not want to be in the brokerage business selling properties at auction, but they had entered the field at an entry level, hoping to become builders, developers or investors, as opposed to being professionals working in real-estate disposition.

"Also, there was no prototype, and I realized that I was a perfect fit to develop the business because it required the same skills that I had learned in my education in law, finance, and business. In legal training, you are given all types of examples and then asked to reconcile them or not reconcile them and apply what law should work and what law should not work, and then you help build a new template. Also the skills needed to succeed in the field fit my personality; I had a knack for people.

"Furthermore, there was a tremendous turnover in firms, because people in the industry had a mentality of not trying to retain top employees. The attitude at that time was each person for himself: 'Get your own deal. Do your own deal. Don't give up fees.' Whereas my attitude from the beginning was if you had a good ability to draw business in for your company, you could get someone else to generate brochures, put signs in the ground, answer phone calls, and do the administrative tasks. But I believed that our top people were not easily replaceable. Also, as we became more successful, the business got more and more complex, requiring a constant upgrading of the caliber of people involved in the business. Therefore, our people must have good judgment in knowing which deals to take and which deals not to take, which approach to take, etc. I believed that the key to growing my business was growing people who could tell our story and then building an infrastructure that could service the business. In 2001, we formed a professional service organization so that our key people can own part of the company's profits. This new professional services partnership was designed to retain and attract the best talent, which would enable us to leap ahead with our plans for dramatic and revolutionary growth. Recently, we have been able to expand our business in terms of the number of people in the firm, the types of projects we handle, and the geography we cover. We now cover over seventy types of properties located throughout the world.

"Last, from the beginning I believed that we were doing something that was unique. I had more confidence than anybody else in the business and have been a very good advocate by never being afraid to ask for business. Because of my strong beliefs, our company had a wider reach and attained a greater volume than anyone else in the industry."

How to Build a Successful Company

Q: You have helped build Sheldon Good & Company into #1 in the field. What guiding principles make business and a professional #1?

GOOD: "I believe there are several key factors that make a company tops in its field; I will first list them and then explain them:

- Establish credibility, ethics, and professionalism
- Develop a good reputation
- Develop a good product
- Provide top customer service
- Value and retain people
- Build long-term relationships
- Build your brand name.

"Credibility, ethics, and professionalism are critical to success today. The first thing that you have to do is be associated with a good company and a good product. One of the big frustrations I have is that many times we may not get a piece of business because one of our competitors oversold what they can do. We know they oversold it. But they figure they've got nothing to lose. Intellectual dishonesty was hard for us to deal with, but what ultimately happened was we have built an outstanding reputation for being the best at what we do and completing every job professionally. Donald Trump once called me 'the best auctioneer in the business.' I am proud of my reputation and that of my firm. As my career has developed, I have found that the character and the competency of the people I am dealing with is everything.

"You must provide excellent customer service whether you are building your career in your own firm or as part of an organization, and from my experience in the auction business that happens only if people are with an industry and a company for a long time. As I stated before, I believe that the key to growing any business is for a company to value you and help you so you can build a long-term career with one organization. Sheldon Good & Company employs many of the same people for a long time.

"Additionally, you should always build your brand name in the marketplace through your people, through the people you choose to do business with you, through publications, and word of mouth."

Q: Whether you choose to move up in an organization or own your own business, what advice would you offer someone on building his or her career?

Lessons Learned

GOOD: "Do several things to be successful:

1. *Expose Yourself to a Broad Base of Jobs.* I learned early that it is good to be exposed to many different kinds of jobs so that you find out what you do and do not like and what fits your talents both ethically and professionally. You should always examine your ethical beliefs in relationship to your field.

2. *Have Something Unique.* It is very important to develop a résumé that distinguishes you from everyone else. The number one question that always ran through my head, and even runs through it today, is 'Why should someone choose you?' If you are in a service business or if you are in a business where people buy your credibility, you must ask yourself, 'Why should they

buy from me rather than my competitors?' Now our specialty is in selling properties through auctions. Years ago, real estate auctions were used as a last resort for properties that were not easily valued. I have believed from the beginning that with turbulent and uncertain market conditions, auctions provide property owners often better solutions than selling their properties in the traditional manner, and we have built a tremendous business reputation of selling properties at auction. Our company is to the real estate business what Sotheby's or Christie's is to the fine art and collectibles business; today, we handle every kind of real estate that can be auctioned. You should find out what you love and what you believe in and then use that information to build your career. Internships and part-time jobs can allow you to learn the business first-hand.

3. *Education Is the Cornerstone of a Good Career.* You have to be able to read, write, and count, and many times you must have the ability to do all three at one time. In addition, I learned that credentialing was also very important. I have kept up my continuing education credits. I am currently licensed in many jurisdictions in the United States.

4. *Network and Build Long-term Relationships.* It is very important to 'network' to make as many friends as you can. I have found that although you never know where friends will end up, they can always help you build your career. And so it becomes a function of meeting people you share a mutual interest with, and at

some point or another, you may be able to help each other. The reason that I chose DePaul Law School is because it had such a strong history of developing well-connected people in Chicago. Better than 95 percent of the graduates from DePaul Law School stay in greater Chicago. I have been very active with DePaul for a long time, and my relationships have helped me in business. You must network constantly and build relationships. Through experience, I have learned that deals come and go, but relationships carry the day. The real estate business is very much a 'who you know' business, as more and more businesses are becoming. So first you must find areas where you have the opportunity to expand your network. Better than a third of the people we do business with here were either former customers or have relationships with customers, vendors, etc. In other words, they were people with whom we already had some connection.

"I believe that you do not need to always have to meet people with a purpose or have a specific goal in mind at the time that you meet them. My experience is that most of the time, you are not quite sure where it will end up, but you should constantly network with others because those networks will add value to your career.

5. *Join Professional Organizations.* I believe that you should join and get involved in a leadership role in professional organizations; it is a valuable way of learning, networking, and making friends.

I am currently the president of the Chicago Association of REALTORS®, a 12,000 member association, the third largest in the United States. I am also the chairman of the National Auction Forum for the National Association of REALTORS®. I have a great time with both of them. I really like the people. I am really interested in what they have to say. I learn a lot from them, and I hope that they learn a lot from me.

6. *Mentors Are Important in One's Career.* I was very fortunate that when I was going through college a number of adults served as mentors to me. They basically took an interest in me and would suggest, 'Why don't you try this or why don't you try that?' And they taught me the importance of philanthropy, charity, giving back, and of not seeking anything in return. I have a good time, and I enjoy meeting people. I also believe in mentoring others; it is a great way to give to others and to your field and to learn.

7. *Have Fun.* I believe in loving what you do and having fun doing it. Sheldon Good & Company has such an interesting story. I am having a great time with it. I believe that you should try to be creative and have a really good sense of humor. Life is so much better if you find a career you enjoy.

8. *Be Optimistic.* You should be optimistic about liking people and having faith in them. When I meet someone and I shake hands with them, I always assume that I am meeting someone who is a nice person. You should not shake hands with someone and believe that they are out to get you.

9. *Write on What You Know.* You will learn, meet people, and build a market niche. I have written for many publications, and recently completed my first of three books for Dearborn Trade Publishing: *Churches, Jails, and Gold Mines ... Mega-Deals from a Real Estate Maverick.* This book is a behind-the-scenes account of some of the most unusual and high stakes real estate deals that Sheldon Good & Company has been involved in. The list of recent deals includes a jail in downtown Indiana, Michael Jordan's restaurant building in Chicago, gold mines in Montana, art deco hotels in South Beach, and Trump Plaza of Palm Beach, Florida. I have worked with Donald Trump, international real estate and business mogul. In fact, he wrote the book's afterword, which contains a story of how he purchased the tallest building in Lower Manhattan for only $4 million in 1995. Now, in 2003 it nets him about $20 million a year in rental profits. Writing helped me clarify my thoughts, get deeper insight, and build my reputation and brand name in the field.

10. *Have a Flexible Business Plan.* You should have a career plan, but I believe that you should be flexible enough to change with the industry and the business climate. When I began working with my father, I did not have a grand plan. When opportunities present themselves, you must have the ability to capitalize on them or else you will lose the opportunity, and someone else can get the opportunity.

11. *Do a Good Job Completely.* I believe in the philosophy that a pro-

fessional must take a 'you can count on me' attitude. Whatever assignment I accept, I know that I need to do it completely. It is very important to do a good job once you are given an opportunity. You have to get on stage and dance the dance or sing the song or do whatever you have to do. You cannot be successful without having the ability to do a good job. There are very few people in life who do what they say they're going to do or do a good job. In other words, do a complete job completely. In a lot of circles, as a result of being capable and being gregarious and doing a good job, you will end up being asked to be on a committee, and then serve on a board, and then perhaps be asked to serve in a leadership position. And it is all because you do a good job and you get along with people and they learn that they can count on you."

Advice from Steve

Q: What suggestions can you make for someone who wants to get a job interview? What would impress you?

GOOD: "First of all, the candidate must know the industry and the firm well enough to discuss the job intelligently at an interview.

"You should develop some type of résumé that distinguishes you from everyone else. Be prepared to tell interviewers why they should hire you, other than you are a nice guy or you're a nice person.

"I am also impressed if you can document that you have done a similar job through internships or other job experiences, because I have found that people's ability to interview for a job and the ability to do the job are two different things. And I have been frustrated at not being able to know whether what someone is telling me is something they can really do. If you have an opportunity to take jobs or internships in your field at anytime in your career, I advise you to do so; it will help build your résumé.

"However, it is even more important to me that someone I know or who is connected with me or our firm recommends you. So remember to use your network throughout your career. And the reality of it is that I've been very fortunate for people having been very kind. And I'm very glad to return the kindness. Therefore, if someone can recommend you in your field, you will have a leg up on others. I have learned that nobody succeeds on his or her own. In other words, there is no such thing as a totally self-made person. It is true that no one is going to make you successful other than you. But someone's going to give you a break. Someone's going to open a door. Someone's going to give you an opportunity. Someone's going to take a liking to you. If anybody in our company gets into a jam, we know how to pick up a phone and help each other. And that is really what it is about. Nobody is bullet-proof. The Beatles got it right: 'You get by doing it with a little help from your friends.'

"Ultimately, once you have the job, then you must walk through that door and use the opportunity to do a complete job both professionally and ethically, because your reputation will lead you to new career opportunities."

Author's Concluding Tips

In summary, although Steven Good had a head start in business by working for his successful father, the way he has built his career and his business are important strategies for you to develop to be successful in your career. Furthermore, Steven offers great advice from a CEO for getting a job and moving ahead in today's business environment. For the past few years that I have covered Steven Good's story, I have seen that he not only moves forward continually in his career, but he also has fun while doing it. If you cannot find something you love and have fun at it, odds are you will not have the energy to be successful. And last, I agree with Steven Good that the Beatles got it right—move forward "with a little help from your friends."

Step 7: Work Hard and Leverage Each Job to Create Your Perfect Career

Interview with Sharon K. Young

"ENJOY THE JOURNEY"

7. Work Hard and Leverage Each Job to Create Your Perfect Career!

6. Put Plan into Action

5. Start a Career Plan

4. Educate Yourself

3. Learn About the Field

2. Examine Your Talents

1. Organize

Drawing by Phil Orlandi

Chapter Seven

Step 7: Work Hard and Leverage Each Job to Create Your Perfect Career

"Leverage each job into a lifetime of career success by working hard; you will end up with a career greater than you dreamed."
—Sharon K. Young

Points to Remember

➤ Learn the value of hard work.

➤ Learn principles of "hard work ethic."

➤ Use failure and success to move forward.

➤ Learn about professional appearance.

➤ Evaluate your career regularly.

➤ Keep your action plan with timetable updated.

You must have heard at least a thousand times on TV about how people volunteered for an activity or hobby they loved at their church, synagogue, children's school, or in their community, and they did such an outstanding job that it led them to a successful career. In my opinion, working hard at whatever job you have, whether it is paid or a volunteer activity, is the most important skill you can have to achieve your perfect career; without it the competition is too hard, and you will not reach your potential. I believe that the universe is affected by your actions, and if they are positive you will eventually benefit from them. You must learn to give 100 percent of yourself in your work-related activities, whether you are being paid or volunteering your services in organizations, at your children's school, at community programs, or religious activities.

Working hard at what you do will enable you to build skills, your portfolio, and earn a reputation for doing a great job, and more often than not you will be rewarded for your work. So often I hear people say, "Well this job is temporary, so I do not care about the work." But trust me: Your reputation will precede you. People know that hard work shows great character.

Learn the Principles of a Hard Work Ethic

It involves many factors:

- Do a complete job to the best of your ability. If you need to, seek expert advice.
- Complete the job on time.
- Do a professional job.
- Look professional; dress the part.
- Take responsibility for your work.
- Provide excellence.
- Take risks, but weigh the risks.
- Build a good reputation.
- Work well as part of a team; learn the skills if you do not have them already.

- Have a good attitude.
- Don't let fear keep you from doing your best.
- Continue to learn.

Each interviewee in this book has built a reputation for doing great work, and that has ended up opening doors for them in their careers that they never would have dreamed of before. For example, Sharon Young now heads two organizations, David Leeds has moved up in his career at Allstate, and Dr. Linneman, in the next story, has built five successful careers simultaneously because in each one he built an outstanding reputation and was asked to be part of new ventures. Dr. Linneman talks about how he started speaking in the field to bring attention to Wharton's Real Estate Program, and he was so good at it that he has been able to build a great side career as a keynote speaker and commentator, which is very financially and personally rewarding for him. So I believe if you take only one thing from this book, it should be this: Work hard at whatever you do and it will lead you forward to places better than you could have imagined.

Use Failure and Success to Move Forward

You will face challenges and obstacles to move forward in your career; everyone does. Since Martha Stewart, Andersen Consulting, and Enron, you are now aware that, overnight, companies may fail. Hopefully, you will never hear the words from Donald Trump made famous in his TV show *The Apprentice*: "You're fired." But, whatever happens in your personal and professional life, you must learn how to use it to move forward. When you get temporarily off course, you must use your experiences as life lessons that will help you move forward. You can do this by evaluating how you have dealt with challenges in your past. For example, if you ever had a weight issue, did you prefer attending Weight Watchers meetings so that you could be around others who had similar issues or would you prefer to deal with it by being by yourself? Most people have a preferred way they deal with challenges such as illnesses, work problems, and family crises. When I counsel adults, I always look for the patterns in their lives. For example, when I have to deal with family illnesses, I always do research, interview others in the situation, learn from the information and experience, and then teach it to others. It is important for you to learn how you prefer to deal with challenges, so that when you experience changes in your industry or world events such as 9/11, you can use the experiences to ultimately move forward. Most successful real estate people I interview often have had to deal with negative balance sheets, but they always look to see how they can make money from it in the future. So if you know how you have dealt with obstacles in your life in previous situations, you can use new ones as opportunities for learning and growth in your career. As you will learn in the next story in this book, Sharon Young has had several successful careers by using challenges as learning lessons to build an even richer and fuller career.

Learn About Professional Appearance

Remember the old saying, "You never get a second chance to make a first impression"? It is really true in a career. Your professional image is important. I suggest that you always dress appropriately, even a little more professionally than others with whom you are working. Even if you work at your church or at your children's school, be sure to always be clean and well groomed and as professionally dressed as possible (in a way that's appropriate for the setting, of course). The point is that you want people to think of you as a confident professional who presents yourself well—it will open doors for you. You need to always keep up with the latest dress codes of your company or in the companies you work with. You may find definitions today of business dress, business casual, and casual dress confusing. Below are a few examples of appropriate and inappropriate attire that should help you better understand how I interpret the new dress code policy so you can achieve a more professional look. And whether we like it or not, just as a book is judged by its cover, so are we. So I always suggest to others to "Dress for Success." To me that means always being more formally dressed than required in the company codes. I believe:

Dress Codes
- Shoulders cannot be exposed.
- Dresses must be an appropriate length.

- Clothing must be in good repair, clean, and pressed, and cannot be torn or ragged.
- Appropriate hosiery or socks are usually a must.
- Shoes or sandals must be worn at all times.
- Open-toed shoes do not look professional.
- For women, revealing clothing and low-cut tops are unacceptable unless you are working in a bar or similar place.

Reflect on and Evaluate Your Career Regularly

You should take time at least once a year to reflect and evaluate your career so that you stay on course and keep your action plan with timetable updated. I developed the next theory of problem solving in my doctorate program from interviewing successful people. They always solved problems in similar steps, so I designed a model to help you to reflect on your career. You can see where the obstacles or roadblocks are, and how to find support, knowledge, etc. so that you can constantly move forward toward your dream career. I want to remind you that even if you are having tremendous success, by using this model and reflecting, you can reach a higher level in your career. Nothing remains static. Change is inevitable and you must be prepared for it. Take time to reflect and evaluate so that you can use your past experiences to serve you. You can repeat these steps every time you want to review how to solve a problem or reach a new high in your career.

Model of Reflection: The Process Involves the Following Steps

1. Conceptualize your next move.

2. Develop a tentative plan.

3. Gather data.

4. Interpret the data.

5. Revise and improve plan.

6. Take action.

7. Evaluate your results and move forward.

Figure 3. Process of Reflection. Your career is a work in progress.

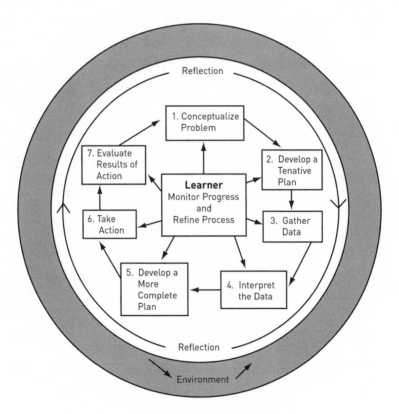

Keep Your Action Plan with Timetable Updated

As the learner, you must move through each process, constantly evolving to reach your goals. As you do new activities such as speaking, writing, volunteering, and getting new ideas, then take time to develop an action plan. As you move forward in each step of the process, you will learn by reflecting on where you have been, where you are, what you have accomplished, and what you need to do next.

Activity: Write My Action Plan

What is my goal?	What will I do to reach it?	When will I do it?	How much time will I devote to it?	What evidence will I use to know if I succeeded?

Interview with Sharon K. Young

This next story centers on a woman who has worked hard her entire career to succeed in six different fields. Sharon Young believes that her hard work ethic has been responsible for her moving forward to new heights. Her career story is one that should illustrate and inspire you to work hard in everything you do so that you can reach for your career goals and beyond. I have learned from successful people like Sharon that working hard will not only bring you success at what you do in the present, but it is also a major component for opening even bigger doors for you in your future.

Biography

Sharon K. Young, CIPS, CRB, CRS, GRI, MBA, CEO, is a member of the Oklahoma City Metropolitan Association of REALTORS® and is president, MLS Gateway. Sharon is a native of Arkansas who has been successful in six different fields since she graduated college. She received both an undergraduate and a graduate degree in business from Wichita State University. Sharon worked for ten years as a plant manager at one of the largest independent jobbing foundries in the world at that time: Grede's Foundry out of Wichita. She has worked for an oil company and she has been an adjunct professor at Oklahoma City University. In 1984, she founded

The First Place Realty, and currently she is the CEO of the Oklahoma City Metropolitan Association of REALTORS®, and the president of MLS Gateway.

She maintains her real estate broker's license in Oklahoma, and she earned several designations and took advanced real estate programs from the National Association of REALTORS®. She is a certified international property specialist (CIPS), a member of the Council of Real Estate Brokers Managers (CRB), a certified residential specialist (CRS), and a graduate of the REALTOR® Institute (GRI). In addition, she is a member of the National Association of REALTORS® (NAR) and the Federation of International Real Estate Professionals (FIABCI).

Six Different Career Fields and Successful at Each

Q: You have had six very successful careers in completely different fields. Please list them.

YOUNG: "Yes, in completely different fields:

1. Directly out of college, I quickly found my 'niche' in corporate America within the oil industry where I was the youngest 'asset manager' in the history of Midwest Oil Corporation.
2. Next, I worked as personnel manager and 'company negotiator' with Demco, Inc., a worldwide manufacturer of valve assemblies.
3. I worked for the Grede Foundries Corporation as a plant manager.
4. I became an adjunct professor at Oklahoma City University. My

subject matter was production management.

5. In 1984, I opened my own real estate company, where I owned and operated two independent real estate offices called The First Place Realty. One was located in Edmond, Oklahoma, and the other in Oklahoma City.

6. Now I am chairman and CEO of Oklahoma City Metropolitan Association of REALTORS® (OKCMAR) and president of MLS Gateway."

Challenges

Q: What were a few challenges that you faced in these positions?

YOUNG: "First I must say that I have always believed that I can eventually turn all my obstacles and challenges into opportunities for growth. So although most of the time, I didn't know *how* my struggles would lead to positive results in my career, I knew that by working hard and doing the best job I could, later on I would benefit from doing the work and building my reputation. Having said that, however, I have had several major challenges:

"Some of my most demanding leadership experiences were gained during my tenure with the Grede Foundries Corporation, then the largest foundry operator in the world. During my near ten-year tenure with Grede, I became the first woman in the history of the American foundry industry to serve as plant manager, responsible for the day-to-day operations of a Class A jobbing foundry with over 400 employees under my leadership. As a woman, I had to learn to deal with problems from a tremendously diverse workforce.

"Another major challenge came when I entered the real-estate industry in 1984 and successfully founded and managed The First Place Realty, in the midst of the worst real estate market in Oklahoma City memory. I had to really focus to financially succeed in that environment. I have subsequently been involved in a wide range of professional, volunteer, and strategic industry activities to help other businesses succeed under turbulent financial situations.

"Then, when I entered my new job as CEO of Oklahoma City Metropolitan Association of REALTORS® (OKCMAR), I had to make a difficult business decision to transfer my ownership in the real estate company to my husband, because I was concerned of a conflict of interest in what I do currently for the Association. I have maintained my broker's license; however, I do not function as a licensed practitioner in real estate at this time, because I believe that you must be above reproach in your business dealings.

"For the past three years, I have been conquering a whole new range of leadership challenges as CEO of the 3,800-customer Oklahoma City Metropolitan Association of REALTORS® and president of MLS Gateway. We have worked to financially position the REALTOR® for success in a new global business environment with all the latest in technology. I have been uniquely successful in bringing together the talents and skills of both leadership and staff to create what is now recognized as one of the most advanced trade association and MLS operations using new technologies in the country."

How Hard Work Leads to Success

Q: Has working hard helped you to reach higher levels in your career?

YOUNG: "I believe that by working hard at each job, I have succeeded at each, and my work ethic has led me to a new path in my career that is even better than the previous one. I believe that the harder I work, the luckier I become in my career and in my life. And every time, working hard and doing the best job I could has opened doors for me and moved me to a higher career place than I could have envisioned. I do believe that success is not an end, but it is a journey, and by working hard you will continue to build throughout your career life to reach your full potential."

Q: Have you learned about the strategy of working hard from other experiences?

YOUNG: "Yes. I once stayed overnight and watched the commander of the USS *Stennis* aircraft carrier, and I realized that the commander really headed a floating organization, and the situation made me think of what being successful in a career and being a CEO ultimately means. It is like running a ship or being a commander at war. And this led me to read many books on the subject such as *The Art of War* by Sunzi et al., *The Book of Leadership and Strategy: Lessons of the Chinese Masters* by Thomas Cleary, and *The Art of War for Executives* by Donald G. Krause. After doing that, I now look at leadership issues in business like they are all about building a strategy as if I were at war."

Q: Do you learn new tactics by reading about aspects of working hard to do a good job?

YOUNG: "I have always loved reading, but today, with events worldwide and new technologies, I must constantly read to keep developing myself and to keep my staff on top of things. I read real estate and business publications such as *The New York Times*, *The Wall Street Journal*, *Crain's*, and *The REALTOR® Magazine* by NAR. I have learned by studying the actions of leaders; my favorites books on the subject are *Jack: Straight from the Gut* by Jack and Suzy Welch, *Jack Welch on Leadership* by Robert Slater, *My American Journey: An Autobiography* by Colin Powell, and *The Leadership Secrets of Colin Powell* by Oren Harari."

Q: Did you have any mentors or role models that helped shape your views on hard work?

YOUNG: "Three people have really been my role models and mentors: my mother, my father, and my husband, Frank.

My mother and father taught me the importance of:

- Having a hard work ethic.
- Judging everyone as an individual by their character, rather than by their race, sex, age, or income.

"My father also taught me about the importance of not quitting. He used to tell me that I should never quit until I had given it my all, because when I give myself permission to quit, the next time it will be easier for me to quit. And if I learn to accept defeat for something, before long I will be accepting failure for myself in many areas. So to this day, I never allow myself to quit until I have achieved my best—then I give myself permission to move on.

"My husband, Frank, taught me the value of treating others with respect, even if I disagree with their business work ethic or decisions. Although I often find this difficult in the moment, I have learned that it is essential in working and getting along with others in an increasingly diverse society. In the words of Harry S. Truman, 'We must build a new world, a far better world—one in which the external dignity of man is respected.' I now believe that we should give each other mutual respect. However, if an employee does not want to work exceptionally hard, then we can disagree about the work; I will treat them with respect, but he or she needs to be on a different team from mine."

What Skills Define Hard Work and Success

Q: As a woman who has reached tremendous success in six different fields and now is a CEO of an organization and president of another at the same time, what skills do you define as part of a "hard work ethic"?

YOUNG: "There are several basic factors that I consider when I examine whether I or someone else is working hard and doing an outstanding job. I believe you must:

1. *Be Passionate About Your Work.* Many times I have been asked, 'Why are you so driven and so passionate about what you are doing?' I do not have an answer other than, 'Why not?' I believe one must be passionate about what one does, and if you read about characteristics of successful people, you will realize passion and energy are always listed. I believe that if you do not believe in what you are doing, no one else will.

2. *Be Present.* The greatest challenge is to concentrate and to be present in the moment, because many times you do not see something coming, and you have to be alert to handle such situations.

3. *Demand Excellence of Yourself.* I believe in the words by Jim Collins in his book *Good to Great*, 'If people accept good, they will never get to great.' I believe firmly that to be successful in your career, you must work hard to demand excellence of yourself by acting like a leader, not a manager. You can start by using ideas

of great leaders. I believe in the ideas in the book *Jack Welch on Leadership* by Robert Slater. Welch, who was CEO of GE, says, 'Stop managing and start leading; to be successful, you must excel, have a vision, and drive its implementation, being able to articulate your vision with energy.' I have learned that a manager asks *how* and *when*, and CEO or leader asks *what* and *why*. A leader envisions and a manager implements. So working hard is about learning to lead by doing your best.

4. *Be Professional.* Integrity and honor are vital to doing a great job. I take nothing personally unless my integrity or character is questioned, since I believe that honor is all that one really possesses. As a mentor and friend said to me: 'Honor is more important than life itself.'

5. *Take Responsibility.* I give people on my team great leeway to build, but with that freedom, I believe, comes responsibility and accountability. I believe in the old saying, 'Actions speak louder than words,' and I always tie that with the words of great leaders. John Quincy Adams said, 'Actions inspire people to take responsibility and demand excellence of themselves and of people with them. Great leaders take responsibility, but require others to also take responsibility.' Winston Churchill said, 'The price of greatness is responsibility.'

6. *Provide Customer Service.* My motto is: 'Excellence is a matter of choice.' In every walk of business life, you compete for that customer. In competing, you must give the customer an

experience greater than what they expect, and that is achieved by excellence, and by being above average, and thinking outside the box. Every time I think about top customer service, I think about a story of customer service at the Ritz Carlton in Chicago. The Ritz Hotel staff is trained to pay attention to detail. They have set the standard for top customer service; no detail is too small.

RITZ CARLTON EXPERIENCE:
The Hood Ornament Story

A businessman had been working so hard in Chicago that he had had no time to clean his car. He had left old wrappings from food he had been eating his car; his car was dirty inside and out, and the hood ornament was crooked from a previous accident.

Without saying anything to the parking attendant at the Ritz, the businessman gave him the car to park so that he could attend a business lunch at the Ritz.

When he picked up his car after lunch, the car was spotless inside and out and the hood ornament had been straightened.

So I always tell people, if you want to know what top customer service is, think about the Ritz and the hood ornament story. If you had a choice of any fine hotel, you would buy the Ritz-Carlton experience. Success comes from keeping abreast of the latest information and services to provide excellence. I believe in the global marketplace. In 2004, I held an international conference for OKCMAR to help REALTORS® learn from people across the globe and experience something outside of their box. Our competition is broader, but likewise so are our opportunities.

7. *Enter Win/Win Relationships.* I believe that we all need to come together as long as it is win-win for all, and this is often possible in business.

8. *Act Like an Entrepreneur.* Even if you are working within an organization, work hard to run it as efficiently as if you owned it. I learned that from Ray Young (not related to me), the owner of TG&Y Stores Company, which had its headquarters in Oklahoma. Ray once told me that he had always watched the costs of doing business. Every night, he would turn off the lights and adjust the heat and air and he advised me to do the same—always take care of my job and the place where I work as if I owned the business. So I treat this business as CEO as if I owned it, and every night I turn off the lights and adjust the heat/air. I am very careful about expenses to this day.

9. *Be Practical.* Theory is good, but to be successful in business, you must develop practical skills such as being responsible for a payroll. In business, you have to put money on the line—it either grows or you lose it. In education, many people have never been in the business field, and have not had the opportunity to learn from someone running a corporation. It is an invaluable

experience to learn from other great leaders such as Winston Churchill. Everything in business is a deal.

10. *Be Flexible to Change.* With new technologies, especially in the real estate arena, the way business is being done is quickly changing to incorporate computers, emails, cell phones, palm pilots, etc. If you do not continue to learn, you will be left behind.

11. *Be a Risk-Taker.* Weigh the risk to see if you think it is worth it for the possible return, but be a risk taker, because nothing in life is safe. I have very much been a risk taker in my career by choosing to work in six completely different fields. I have always analyzed the risk first to see if it made sense before taking on the new challenge, but I have always been pleased with the end result. I value thinking outside the box and taking action. As Jack Welch said, 'I have no problems with people who come to me with big plans or big dreams, big stuff. They know we're not going to nail them because they didn't make their plan. We are going to reward them for getting close to the plan they wanted in the context of the environment they're in.' (from *Jack Welch on Leadership* by Robert Slater, p. 104). I believe the edge comes when you have to do new things, have conviction, and you make it happen.

12. *Learn How to Build Teams.* People do not build great careers by themselves. I believe that a person who is a leader, whether it is on their own or working for an organization, can work well

as part of a team. You must act more like the conductor of an orchestra, and your role is to utilize every member to contribute as a team to make beautiful music so it sounds like the best symphony.

13. *Learn to Work Smarter, Not Just Harder.* I take time each year to reflect so that I can do a better job and reenergize myself. Otherwise I will lose my edge. So I like to stop and think about my career once a year. I keep a journal, and I review it to write an action plan for the future. I try to find an activity that allows me to view my career with new eyes. Years ago, I got my pilot's license, because I found that when I take off in a plane, I feel as though I have left everything behind. When I am in the air, I see the world from a different perspective, and I am able to learn new ideas to push the envelope. Life is an adventure. I believe in the words of Jack Welch, 'To be successful you need to find new ways to open your eyes to different perspectives in order to think outside the box.'"

Do Not Allow Fear to Stop You

Q: Has fear ever affected your going for a new position in your career?

YOUNG: "Of course I have had fears in going from one field into a completely different field, but I do not allow fear to stop me or paralyze me. I believe that if I concentrated on my fear, my greatest fear would become my reality. I do not believe in problems in life, but just opportunities for growth. I have a saying I live by: 'This too shall pass.' I believe whole heartedly that working hard and reaching for goals is not about being safe, but you have to believe in yourself, in your mission and vision, and the greater good in the universe. Fear can be paralyzing. You must trust that if you work hard, you do not have to know where you are going, but by being present and working hard to the best of your abilities, it will lead to opportunities. I do not believe in being pessimistic. In the short-term, you may reach for something or you may have to make unpopular decisions and you should be prepared to suffer the consequences, such as losing your position or your investment. But in the long run you will grow, and it will lead you to a lifetime of career success."

Advice on Success from Sharon

Q: What advice would you offer others on finding their perfect job/career? What are some of the main qualities you look for in a person when trying to hire someone for a job?

YOUNG: "I would say that attitude is one of the main things I look for when hiring someone. You can teach people skills, but it is most difficult to teach them work ethic. My experience is that if they have a good work ethic, the rest you can create by investing in training for them. If two people apply for a job with me, and one has better skills, and the other one has better background and experiences showing a good work ethic, then I give greater weight to the person with the good work ethic.

"I do look at professional appearance. It is very important for people to look professional and wear proper attire for their position. I always tell my employees to 'Dress for Success.' Whether you like it or not, people do form their initial opinion of you by the way you are dressed. We do judge the book by the cover, and I want people associated with me to look professional. I also think that when people dress too casually, it can influence how they act in the job. For example, in the summertime, I do not permit open-toed shoes in the office. I do have a dress code in the office, and people should learn what is expected of them in an organization before applying for a position.

"Many factors will make up your ability to do a great job. I cannot stress enough that you must be well-grounded, work smart, build on your skills, be passionate, persevere, display team willingness, accountability, a win-win philosophy, and work hard for the betterment of the universe. We are living in a global economy and people don't realize how what they do influences the entire universe. If you do the right things, you will be unbeatable. How you act will come back to you, for good or bad. I believe in the words that inspired me, 'You can be unstoppable,' in a book titled, *Unstoppable: 45 Powerful Stories of Perseverance and Triumph from People Just Like You*, by Cynthia Kersey.

You need to keep moving forward by working hard at every job, and it will lead you to a lifetime of career opportunities. I believe in the words of John Quincy Adams:

"Inspire people to dream more, learn more,
do more and become more."

Author's Concluding Tip

In summary, Sharon Young's story illustrates how, by working hard and using the tactics she set forth in this chapter, she has been successful in six different fields and it has opened doors for her she never expected. I believe that if you follow the steps in the book, and work hard at it, it will lead you to where you need to be—an even higher place than you can envision. You cannot underestimate the value of working hard in everything you do for your future success. The next chapter will sum up the key points in this book and give you a philosophy to guide your future.

Conclusion:

Putting It All Together
and "Enjoying the Journey"

Interview with Dr. Peter Linneman

"ENJOY THE JOURNEY"

7. Work Hard and Leverage
Each Job to Create Your
Perfect Career!

6. Put Plan into Action

5. Start a Career Plan

4. Educate Yourself

3. Learn About the Field

2. Examine Your Talents

1. Organize

*Drawing by
Phil Orlandi*

Chapter Eight

Conclusion: Putting It All Together and "Enjoying the Journey"

"A good career is a journey, not a destination. Know where the stops are, but enjoy the journey."

—Dr. Peter Linneman

Points to Remember

➤ Follow the seven steps to success.

➤ Use challenges and obstacles to move toward success.

➤ Learn to reflect and evaluate your career regularly.

➤ Keep action plan updated.

➤ Keep building your portfolio.

➤ Follow the skills daily for success.

➤ Enjoy the journey.

Follow the seven steps in this book to set yourself on the road to success. We all have challenges and crises, but successful people use everything to move forward. They know that each step will help them build their house on a solid foundation—such an attitude is truly a blueprint for success.

When you begin, remember that getting started is the hardest part of all. Once you start, focus on only one of the seven steps at a time, and try to complete the step as well as you can before moving to the next step. The more you develop each step, the more solid the foundation on which you build your house. The process may sound simple as explained by very successful people, but simple does not mean easy. However, if you are determined, work hard, and maintain your focus on where you are in the process of the 7 Steps, you can and will move forward, regardless of events in your life and in the world.

Learn to Reflect and Evaluate Your Career Regularly

At least once a year, I recommend that you take time to reflect and evaluate: Where have you been? Where are you now? What have you accomplished and what do you need to do to move forward? And then design a plan. Celebrate your accomplishments and know that as long as you are alive you can move forward! So think positively. This is what I do each year:

My New Year's Resolution
Time to Reflect and Celebrate

Each December, right before New Year's Eve, I take a moment to reflect on my work accomplishments that year, and then I jot down on paper a few thoughts. At my New Year's Eve celebration, I celebrate only my accomplishments, not what I will do next. I do that work after New Year's Eve.

1. What have I accomplished?
2. What was I really thrilled that I did this year?
3. What new risks did I take?

As January begins, you need to go over your notes and take time to reflect on your career. Unfortunately, you may tend to focus on what you have not accomplished in your career. I found in studying successful people that they always turn any negatives in their career that year and they reframe it in their mind to make it a positive; to them the *glass is always half-full, not half-empty*. You must try to see the world as being full of opportunities, and if you are willing to do the work, and follow the "7 Step Process", you will have success.

At this point, you may need to revisit what you really value after reading this book. I found that Maslow's theory really will apply to how you examine your values as you move up in your career. Abraham Maslow (1970), *Motivation and Personality*, 2nd ed., Harper & Row, is known for establishing the theory of a hierarchy of needs. According to Maslow (1970), human beings are motivated by unsatisfied needs, and that they must satisfy certain lower needs before higher needs can be satisfied. He felt that people are basically trustworthy, self-protecting, and self-governing and that humans tend toward growth and love. Maslow believed that once you satisfy your basic needs, such as hunger, higher needs will emerge as important in your life, and then these needs, rather than physiological needs, will become more essential in your life. Maslow studied exemplary people, such as Albert Einstein, Jane Addams, and Eleanor Roosevelt. Basically, Maslow (1970) categorized needs in the above chart and with explanation below. In Maslow's

Figure 4. Maslow's Hierarchy of Needs

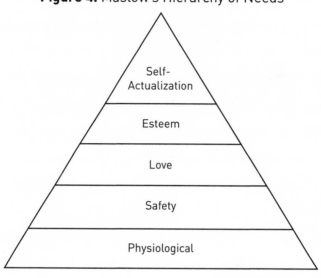

hierarchy of needs, it is assumed that lower order (deficit) needs are first met before you rise to the next level:

Physiological Needs

Human beings must satisfy their basic physiological needs such as air, food, water, sleep, sex, etc.

Safety Needs

When all physiological needs are satisfied and no longer controlling adults' thoughts, then they become aware of their safety. Safety is mostly psychological in nature and has to do with establishing stability and consistency in a chaotic world. We need the security of a home and family. For example, if a woman has an abusive husband, she cannot move to the next level because she is constantly concerned for her safety.

Love Needs

Human beings have a desire to be loved and affiliated with others (e.g., clubs, work groups, religious groups, family, gangs, etc.).

Esteem Needs

Adults need to achieve competence and gain approval and recognition.

Self-Actualization

Once all other needs are met, "adults desire to become everything that one is capable of becoming." People at this level seek knowledge, peace, esthetic experiences, self-fulfillment, and oneness with God, and so forth.

As you move forward in your career, you might want to reevaluate your main goals, values, and purpose for work. I found that most people will decide on how to pursue their career once they are successful in a field so that they make the most of it. For example, Jennifer Ames today is creating a more balanced and healthier lifestyle now that her business is successful. Dr. Linneman pursued several different career paths once he was successful as a professor in order to satisfy all his personal needs and values in his career. David Leeds is now pursuing an education so he can later teach returning adults and give back what he has learned. All interviewees in this book valued the needs listed below, and have generally been able to reach the following needs. At this time, you need to circle which ones you have reached, and write a short sentence next to the ones you would like to fulfill in the future.

Activity: I Have Fulfilled the Following Needs:

1. Financial Success_____

2. Loving My Work _____

3. Quality of Life, Such as Independence and Control _____

4. Building Relationships _____

5. Continued Growth of My Businesses _____

6. Client Satisfaction _____

7. New Opportunities for Growth _____

8. Having Fun _____

9. Staying Healthy by Balancing My Life/Work _____

10. Others _____

Process of Reflection

This last activity is for you to again reflect on where you are now in your career, where you want to be, and how you will satisfy your needs and values that you listed above. Challenge yourself to think about how you fit in the overall world. Look at your career, your target business market, and changes that are happening in the world that will affect your career. It is important to have a perfect fit. As Patricia Choi said, she was in the right place, at the right time, to have the right opportunity to use her talents. You must constantly see the bigger picture so that you can change and learn to be successful in your career. Three areas you must fit to be successful are: your talents, your organization/context, and the world. The next diagram should make you think about how you fit in the overall picture. The first circle represents you; the second, your organization; and the third, how you fit into the overall world.

Figure 5. Three Circles of How You Fit

1. Your Talents

2. Your Organization/Context

3. The World

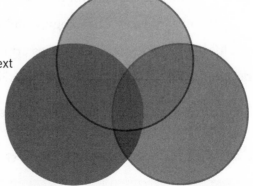

Then, once you have reflected and thought about your next year, you should write a specific action plan.

Activity: My Action Plan

Specific Action Steps I Want to Take	My Next Moves	Time Frame	How I Will Measure My Success

In the past seven years, I have interviewed more than two hundred people about their success in school and in business in a wide variety of fields, including human resource development, banking, real estate, information technology, training, teaching, and consulting. I found that a few key strategies applied to people in all fields who were successful, regardless of age, sex, or background. I list these strategies at the end of this chapter.

I also found the strategies were the same ones Dr. Linneman shared with me in his interview for a chapter I wrote on how he built his consulting career in the top-selling book by the American Society of Training and Development (ASTD) titled, *Building a Successful Consulting Practice* (2002). His chapter was called, "Establishing a World-Renowned Consulting Business: Linneman Associates."

In addition to Linneman's consulting, he is a practitioner, speaker, writer, author, and full-time professor at Wharton where he mentors students in the program. Because he has been so successful in five fields simultaneously and because he regularly offers advice to students on their careers, I knew he could offer you valuable information on finding and building your perfect career. So I contacted Dr. Linneman again to ask him if he would tell his story, offer his advice on career success, and describe his career/life philosophy for this book.

Dr. Linneman's answers will provide you with enormous insight on his views regarding each of his five career fields, the top skills and strategies he believes you must develop to succeed, and the philosophy that both he and I believe in passionately. Although he will discuss his philosophy in detail at the end of this chapter, in short, Dr. Linneman believes that although you can expect to have crises, challenges, and changes during your career, you should move forward regardless of what happens in your life, because "A career is a journey, not a destination. Know where the stops are in your career and in your life. Enjoy the journey."

Interview with Dr. Peter Linneman

Dr. Linneman is a full-time professor in the real estate program at the Wharton School, University of Pennsylvania, Philadelphia, PA, a world-renowned consultant of Linneman Associates, a successful practitioner, a well-known keynote speaker and commentator, a writer, and also an author.

Biography

Dr. Peter Linneman is the principal of Linneman Associates, a consulting firm located in Philadelphia, PA. He formed Linneman Associates in 1978 through which he has been a consultant to U.S. and international companies and universities in all areas of their business. For more than twenty-five years, he has provided strategic and financial advice to leading corporations and universities. Dr. Linneman is known internationally as a consultant on real estate, finance, and investments, as well as general business strategy, financial analysis, and human strategy. At universities, he has been involved in the creation of real estate programs where he has consulted on a wide range of areas such as the development of programs, design of curriculum, hiring of staff, acquisition of students, and marketing of the programs. When Dr. Linneman began his practice, he mainly consulted on antitrust litigation. His practice has evolved and changed over the years so that he advises clients on all areas of their business. His clients have included Lubert-Adler Investments, Equity International Properties, Sunbelt Management, General Electric Capital Corporation, GMAC, IBM, Michelin Tire, University of Colorado, Johns Hopkins University, and Roosevelt University.

Dr. Peter Linneman holds both Master's and Doctorate degrees in economics from the University of Chicago. In 1977, he was a post-doctoral fellow in economics at the Center for the Study of the Economy and the State at the University of Chicago. In 1978, he became the assistant professor of business economics at the Graduate School of Business, University of Chicago. From 1979 through 1984, he was the assistant professor of finance and public policy at Wharton School, University of Pennsylvania. In 1984, Linneman became an associate professor of finance and public policy at Wharton, and in 1988, he was appointed as professor of finance and public policy at Wharton. Dr. Linneman is the Albert Sussman Professor of Real Estate professor of finance and public policy and management at the Samuel Zell and Robert Lurie Real Estate Center at the Wharton School, University of Pennsylvania, where he was the director of the center from 1985 through 1998. Dr. Linneman was appointed chairperson, Wharton Real Estate Department from 1994-1997 and named Albert Sussman Professor of Real Estate in 1989. The Wharton program is regularly identified as the top program in real estate, and Dr. Linneman is credited as a major contributor to the program's success. He continues to teach full-time at

Wharton, and he is the editor of the *Wharton Real Estate Review*. He has published more than seventy articles, and is author of a new textbook, *Real Estate Finance & Investments: Risk and Opportunities,* and *The Linneman Letter,* a leading economic and real estate strategy research publication. He is regularly a keynote speaker and moderator for leading corporations and professional associations around the world.

Linneman Attends College

Q: Where did you grow up?

LINNEMAN: "I was born in Kentucky, across the river from Cincinnati, in the Cincinnati metropolitan area. We moved when I was a very small child to Lima, Ohio, which was a classic, rust-belt, Ford Motors, Westinghouse, U.S. Steel, Standard Oil of Ohio kind of place."

Q: You went to college to play football?

LINNEMAN: "I went to Ashland College, not to play football, but I chose which college I was going to attend based on where I thought I would play the most and have the best opportunity."

Q: What career or field did you plan to follow after college, and how did you get into teaching?

LINNEMAN: "I had no idea what I wanted to be when I entered college other than perhaps a lawyer, only because that was what I thought you did if you went to college. I didn't even know what an economics course or a business degree was at that time—remember I came from a blue-collar family. An economics course was just on my schedule, and I met an extraordinary woman by the name of Dr. Lucille Ford, my teacher in economics, and she turned me on to economics and on becoming a professor. She has been my mentor, and has become a lifelong dear friend. We have funded a speaker series at Ashland in her name and in recognition of her contributions.

"Also, I met my wife, Kathy, the first day in orientation, and the rest, as they say, is history. We have been married almost thirty-one years and together thirty-five. She was in elementary education and has supported my interest in teaching and other career developments. For our honeymoon, we drove to the University of Chicago for me to apply for graduate school after I received my B.A. in economics and political science from Ashland."

Q: Why did you select the University of Chicago graduate school for a degree in economics?

LINNEMAN: "I really liked economics from the first day I took the course with Lucille Ford; it made sense to me. And Lucille and two other faculty members had told me that I had a certain degree of aptitude for it and suggested that I go to graduate school. I applied at the University of Chicago and was accepted."

Linneman Becomes a Professor

Q: How did you decide to pursue teaching in real estate?

LINNEMAN: "In the beginning at University of Chicago, I took microeconomics, macroeconomics, and labor economics. Then, several professors at the University helped me do research and start teaching at the University of Chicago in their economics department and business school: Milton Friedman, George Stigler, Ted Schultz, Gary Becker, George Tolley, and Jim Heckman, who was also part of my doctoral committee. These professors helped me complete both my degrees in less than four years. Many of these professors went on to win a Nobel Prize."

Q: How did you decide to teach at Wharton?

LINNEMAN: "It was a very hard decision. Two universities got into 'a bidding contest.' University of Chicago was offering $23,000 and Wharton offered $23,500, and as I look back at it, I laugh that it actually entered into my thought process. Well, it was a lot of money then, but I was more excited that at my young age I had the University of Chicago and Wharton bidding on me.

"The message I have since told students is that a one or two percent difference is not a lot of money on which to base a career. For me, I was probably emotionally ready for a change after being in Chicago for six years. Not because I disliked Chicago—quite the opposite. I love the city and University of Chicago. But I think emotionally, I knew I could do it in Chicago, but I wanted do know if I could do it elsewhere. Not that I was under a shadow, but on the other hand, there is something to being out on your own and making your way and knowing it wasn't due to your protectors.

"But I do say to students to this day, 'You are going to look back thirty or forty years from now and laugh at yourself—not that you made the wrong decision, but that you actually let that small a number of dollars enter into the decision process, as opposed to where will you be most productive, where you will be happiest, where you will make the most difference, and add the most value in your career.'"

Q: Many adults do not realize that they can fulfill all of their values and needs by following several paths at once. You have pursued five different careers as a professor, consultant, practitioner, speaker/moderator, writer, and now author. In the next section, please explain: Why you chose each field, how each one came about, and what each offered you as part of your career. First, what were you looking for in teaching?

LINNEMAN: "I am still a full-time faculty member at Wharton, but I do not run the program anymore. I teach a normal load of three courses a year. Most professors average about fifty students per class, and I have about ninety students in each.

I obviously like three things about teaching:

- *I Really Value Learning.* I like knowledge for the sake of just knowing things.

- *I Like Being Told I Am Right.* In teaching or academia, you have that luxury. Given the choice of a million dollars or being told by somebody I respect that I am right, I would always pick the latter. I love to be right. Larry Summers, who was using the foundation of government as an example, once said this very well: 'In academia, if you are working on a problem and you cannot figure out the right answer, you study it another three months. In business or government, you have to make a decision and you know it is going to be a wrong decision. The only question is what is the better wrong decision?' And that, I think, is the part of me that likes academia—that I really value being right.

- *I Value Teaching My Knowledge to Others and Helping Them With Their Careers.* Obviously, I do enjoy teaching in places like Chicago and Wharton, where you are not exactly in the blackboard jungle. And I wanted to help students who want a career in the field learn two factors that are so important in a career choice: 'Know who you are and what you value.' I think that that comes hard to everybody, because we all want to be somebody else. I think most people walk down the street saying, 'I want to be the person on the other side of the street.' I always had an amazing arrogance, even in my youth, and I am very happy being me. I wish I understood why some do and some don't have it, and then I could help others understand that concept and help them find the best answers for themselves."

Linneman on Becoming a Consultant

Q: How did you enter into consulting?

LINNEMAN: "Almost immediately after I started teaching, through recommendations, I began consulting as a sideline for Michelin Tire Company and Scott Paper. Both my consulting practice and my teaching career have prospered ever since. I have always been allowed to do other things in my career outside of working for the university as long as it did not interfere with my productivity, which it never has, and both careers add value to my ability to be more effective at each."

Q: Why did you believe you had the expertise to be a successful consultant?

LINNEMAN: "From the beginning, I knew a great deal of relevant theory, and I always had complete confidence in my ability to deliver valuable information to clients. However, like anything else in life, when first people come to you, you pretend you are very experienced in what you are doing, and you wing it as you go. In retrospect, I was able to frame their problems in the context of theory, devise practical ways to research their position, along with an explanation of what it would mean to their business."

Q: And what did consulting offer you that being a pure academic did not?

LINNEMAN: "Consulting offered me several things:

- It offered me a better lifestyle because it was much more re-munerative. I live a decent lifestyle and make a decent living, mostly due to consulting.
- It gave my career life a balance. Even high-speed academia is slow. And so over the last twenty-seven years, consulting has given me connectivity, adrenaline, activity, and access. I like ac-tion and the adrenaline I get in consulting as apposed to aca-demia, which is very, very slow.
- I found the decisions that businesses had to make difficult, but very interesting.
- Consulting gave me access to real senior decision-makers, CEOs presidents, and EVPs and allowed me to have input on their decisions so that I could share that information with other aca-demics and with young people who thirty years from now will be decision-makers. Consulting helps me have an impact with

what I'm doing as a professor. I like to think I know information that is useful and I like to be part of that process.

- Consulting gave me the opportunity to be wrong, but to adjust. If academia gives me the luxury of not being wrong, business gives me the opportunity to be wrong, and then to adjust to it. A few years ago, I took the time out from teaching and went to work with Sam Zell for about fourteen or fifteen months, which was terrific, and I traveled to help him build his new company. I made a million mistakes, but I did some good things, and I was able to help him build Equity International LLC. I learned and enjoyed the experience, although traveling that many miles on airplanes was very challenging when you are as tall as I am (I am 6'4").

- I believe that consulting has added to my being a much better teacher. It made me learn how not to say simple things in a complicated manner. Often in graduate school it seems that professors take simple concepts and make them sound very complicated. And in reality, communication and learning is all about the opposite. It is how to take complicated things and make them extremely clear, simple, and persuasive. And I love that; I think one of the great frustrations I have in academia is that people don't take on that challenge with their students, their writing, or even in their consulting. There are many exceptions, Larry Summers and Milton Friedman for example, but in general that does not happen, and I really value that.

- I have built great long-lasting relationships, such as with Sam Zell."

Linneman Becomes a Well-Known Speaker

Q: You became a well-known keynote speaker around the world. How did that start and why do you think you are so good at it?

LINNEMAN: "I started speaking in the '80s because I wanted Wharton to be identified as the place to learn about real estate. I simply wanted to bring people to Wharton. I did not start speaking to make money, but it has turned out to be quite remunerative. I have good speaking and communication skills. I am better at the spoken word than I am the written word."

Q: Why do you like speaking?

LINNEMAN: "I enjoy speaking because I am in control of the end result. I get to tell people a story with the utmost conviction that I believe I am right; nobody in life normally allows people that freedom except to a speaker. All I have to do is decide what story I want to tell this particular audience.

"Also, I love the challenge of taking complicated ideas and results and making them understandable to intelligent people who are not in my area of expertise. The analogy I always use is, nobody in their right mind would ever buy a television based upon a salesperson's going through technical specifications about why a television works and gamma rays. I don't care how intelligent you are. The challenge is how to take this very complicated piece of physics and engineering that yields a television and sell it to you by saying, 'Push this button and it comes on, and you use this button to change the color, and this button if you want to change the channel.' That is the challenge, and I love that challenge."

Linneman Becomes a Well-Known Moderator

Q: You became well known as a moderator at large conferences. How did that start and why have you been so successful at it?

LINNEMAN: "Later on, from speaking, I was asked to moderate several conferences, and I have built a nice niche. For example, each year for the past fourteen years I have moderated a real-estate roundtable conference by invitation only for Sam Zell and Marshall Bennett that brings in very high-level people. It is called 'The Marshall Bennett Classic.' I became a good moderator, because I know a fair amount of information and I have a little bit of glibness, but I am not offensive. When I am a moderator, I always approach it as, 'What is the story I want to have told and how do I get the people who I am moderating to tell the story I want to tell?' When you are giving a speech, you are painting the picture. When you are moderating, it comes out a bit choppier, but the challenge is to make it come out like a mosaic more than a picture.

So when you are moderating several people, you are listening to them talk, and I find that is interesting. If you think about what Oprah Winfrey is good at, she is creating this mosaic so the audience believes that they got the story. I find that very fun and very challenging."

Linneman Becomes a Successful Practitioner

Q: You have also been able to be very successful as a practitioner.

LINNEMAN: "Yes. I learned that I have some business acumen, and I have been successful at many endeavors such as:

- I served as chairman of the board of Rockefeller Center Properties, the public real estate investment trust that until 1996 held the debt on New York City's Rockefeller Center.
- I have bought and sold a strategic block of stock and made money in Israel and other places around the world.
- I served as senior managing director of Equity International Properties, a global real estate investment firm.
- I also served on the board of directors of seven NYSE firms and one Tel Aviv Exchange company. I have served on the boards of numerous private companies.
- I worked with Sam Zell to help him establish Equity International LLC."

Q: Describe how you got involved as a practitioner.

LINNEMAN: "My involvement as a practitioner always occurred when I had a consulting assignment, and through the circumstances of my consulting, it resulted in my becoming a practitioner. I always enjoyed it because it gave me action. For example, I served as chairman of the board of Rockefeller Center Properties, the public real estate investment trust that until 1996 held the debt on New York City's Rockefeller Center. In this capacity, I was active in the process of foreclosing on its Japanese owners and the successful sale of Rockefeller Center. I had originally been a board member, and after a series of events, I became chairman at the same time—we held the mortgage. And at the same time, the Japanese decided they didn't want to pay the mortgage at all, and so, I took over the day-to-day responsibility."

Q: Why have you been so successful and what do you like about it?

LINNEMAN: "I was successful as a practitioner, because I always understood the difference between being an advisor and a principal. A principal has to make decisions, knowing he or she can be wrong. And an advisor has the luxury of saying why it is going to be a wrong decision. And although I am very good at being an advisor, I learned I also liked being on the other side because I was willing to make what I felt was the *best* wrong decision and then adjust two or three months later. For example, I had a fiduciary responsibility as chairman in the Rockefeller deal. People had entrusted me, and I believe we had a good outcome, because the shareholders had a good value creation out of it. I also enjoyed the exercise of it because it gave me action."

Q: What did you learn from being a practitioner that you *didn't* like about it that ultimately changed your career decisions for your future?

LINNEMAN: "I worked with Sam Zell to help him establish Equity International LLC a few years ago. I was on the road with Sam for about fourteen months traveling all over the world, and I learned with Sam what it takes to run that type of organization. I admire people enormously, like Sam and also Doug Crocker, who was CEO of Equity Residential, the largest owner of apartments in the U.S., in seeing what it takes to be so successful and what the care and feeding of employees, including very senior employees, required. I think the time that I spent with Sam Zell helped me really learn a lot about myself. I have great admiration for people who can do that in the same way that I have great admiration for people who can play basketball extraordinarily well. But I learned that is just not what I want to do. Until the experience with Sam, I did not real-ize to the fullest extent that I just didn't want to run a great deal of people. It was the H.R. issues. It was the care and feeding. People who can do it deserve the salaries they get because if you can make

40,000 employees 2 percent more productive, that's staggering value in creation. And what I found is, it is just not what I enjoy. So I have had a number of opportunities to become president or CEO of companies, but I turned them down, because I didn't want to run people. I do not really have the appetite to wake up every morning and say there are 442 mouths waiting for me to tell them what to do; it was not for me."

Q: At one point in your career, you became chair of Wharton's Real Estate Department and you also were appointed director of the Samuel Zell and Robert Lurie Center. You must have been responsible for many people in those positions.

LINNEMAN: "Yes. And before I had been running the Wharton program, I had on my private consulting side, two or three people who work for me, and I also have served on some of the boards at different companies such as Sam Zell's and others, and I have had several other business ventures. However, as I look back, the people part of it is the part of it that I least enjoyed. People often ask me, 'Why don't you hire a bunch of these bright young kids out of Wharton and put them on your payroll and build a larger business?' But working with Sam, at one point, and through my other experiences, I have examined this issue several times in my career, but my answer is always no, because I do not want to manage them."

Linneman Is Also a Well-Known Writer and Now Author

Q: You have become established as a well-known writer and now author. How did that start?

LINNEMAN: "I first published a paper while I was still in graduate school. And I have continued to write over the years:

- I have written over seventy papers in my career.

- I write a lot in the *Wharton Real Estate Review*.

- I have the *Linneman Letter*. As part of Linneman Associates, I have a couple of partners who have worked with me to publish the *Linneman Letter* since 2001. A subscriber typically pays $12,000 per year. Largely, my partners take care of the managerial part of that. Obviously, I have to interact with my partners, but that is a very different exercise. My partners take care of the people and process part of the *Linneman Letter*.

- I have recently published a textbook, *Real Estate Finance & Investments: Risk and Opportunities*. I decided not to use a publisher, because I did not think they added enough value. They take 80 to 90 percent of the revenue. I believe that publishers are probably better at it than me; I just do not believe that they are 80 percent of the value. I knew that I had the staff and business acumen to figure out how to design and market the book successfully."

Q: What does being an author/writer give you that the other fields don't?

LINNEMAN: "Writing has benefited me in several ways:

1. I gained access and built relationships with high-level business people.

2. I have been able to have an impact on my field through writing. I learned to write in a way that both students and high-level business people understood the information. My writing may not fit the model in typical academia, but I learned how to develop a format where my business audience could understand the information. I now have had the good fortune that there are major people, whether it is Sam Zell, or the CEO of Equity One, or Dean Adler of Lubert-Adler reading my newsletter. I know they read it because they pay for it. And once you get major people in your field reading your material, then I feel you have a responsibility to write it in a way they can understand the information. It would be as if you actually knew that the President of the United States would read your papers—and then you refuse to write them in a language he can understand. And so my view is that I have struggled my entire career to get access to where these people will read my material and once I reached the point that they will read it, then I have a responsibility to write it in a format that they can read and that has been enormously rewarding. Three examples I can give are: (1) I wrote a piece in *Wharton Real Estate Review,* 'The Forces Changing Real Estate Forever,' (2) a paper that I did with Debbie Moy in which we looked at the returns to REITs vs. opportunity funds vs. core

real estate. I am told that that paper had a lot of impact with real investors making decisions about real money—hundreds of millions of dollars. And (3), the paper I did on 'Should REITs be included in the S&P 500?' was written a month before that decision was made on whether REITs should go in the S&P 500 and, I was told, that it was heavily read and analyzed by S&P 500 in making that decision. I have really worked my entire career to have access to the people we all hope to impact.

3. It has been fun to share my knowledge with others and have fun writing. The cute thing in the book is basically every building that is mentioned is a person that, when they read it, knows it is them. I named sites like the Kathy Center, obviously for my wife, and my mother's, my goddaughters', and a couple of TAs who were helping me on this all have their names in the book. Again, I have some fun while working seriously on a project—it is a theme throughout my career."

Q: How did you develop your talent at writing in becoming an author?

LINNEMAN: "I have become better over the years. It is constant work. There is no 'Eureka.' Just draft, after draft, after draft. I found over years of teaching that there was no decent textbook, in my opinion, for my students and I thought they should have something. Originally I thought that I was just going to tape my lectures and make the notes available to students. And then as it developed, I thought 'Why don't we publish a textbook?' And then I made the self-publishing decision. I had two fabulous students who had taken the course the year before who helped me."

Q: What have been your biggest challenges you faced in your career?

LINNEMAN: "I would say I have had two major challenges: One of my biggest challenges in my career has always been to assess my time correctly to be able to complete outstanding work on time. This was a major problem when I became chairman of the board of the company that owned the loan on the Rockefeller Center. I assessed that it might take five to eight days per year, and within eight months, the situation had changed dramatically, and it was suddenly going to take 1,000 to 1,100 hours in the next year. The difficulty in that situation was not the task, but the misassessment of the time that it was going to take to complete the job.

"Second, I believe that my reputation is very important. I have found over the years that I have put my trust into people that my intuition had told me not to trust. However, I still trusted them, and in the end, they turned out not to be reliable. I would still have to complete a professional job that I had counted on them to complete, because in the end, all you have is your reputation."

Q: I know when you first went into consulting, you told me you did so because you valued the independence and control it gave you. Would you still say those are your top priorities? Please explain how would you define success for you today.

LINNEMAN: "I still value independence and control, but today my definition of success has evolved and I want more things in addition, including:

1. Have fun
2. Stay healthy by balancing my life/work
3. Have financial success
4. Love my work
5. Build relationships
6. Continue the growth of my businesses
7. Maintain client satisfaction
8. Initiate new opportunities for growth
9. And of course, quality of life, such as independence and control.

"Donna Moore, Richard Rainwater's wife, is an impressive person, and I had her to the campus about three years ago to give a speech. And she said, 'The greatest luxury in life is really freedom and independence in what you do.' Obviously, we treasure it in a societal sense, but I think in an individual sense also. And I have the luxury of a degree of freedom by pursuing five fields in totality that fulfill all my career values and expectations. I had the skills required to be effective in each field, and each career came out of the hard work, my reputation, and my abilities. I do not think that I would have stayed in university for over twenty-five years, had I not done the business stuff on the side. But, by being in different fields, I have been able to satisfy all my career goals and values, although I should say, I do not have any children, so I was able to spend more time on my career than most people with large families."

Q: What's next for you personally in your career?

LINNEMAN: "There are four things I would like to accomplish in the next five years:

- *Continue to Have fun and Love My Work.*
- *Do New Things.* If you would have asked me five years ago if I would be doing the *Linneman Letter* or a book, I would have said absolutely not. I really hope that if you came back five years from now, there would be two or three more things that I would have never dreamed I would be doing that I'm doing. That's been true my entire career.
- *Build My Business Ventures.* I have a couple of ideas, of business-related ideas that I am exploring with some people and hopefully they will come to fruition. And if they don't, something else will come to fruition.
- *Take Time Off to Travel.* I want to travel more by taking my family members on trips."

Lessons Learned

Q: From your experiences in building a successful career in five different fields, what strategies do you think are essential for someone to succeed today, regardless of what field they are in?

LINNEMAN: "There are several important strategies you need to employ to be successful:

1. *Know Yourself Well.* The sooner you can figure out what you are extraordinary at, the better you can exploit your talents. And I think most people don't really ask themselves, 'Why am I succeeding and what am I good at?' I didn't really focus on the fact that I did not particularly enjoy managing people until relatively late in my career. And if I would have understood that better, I think I would have made decisions that better fit my talents. And imagine if you were the world's fastest person, but you were out in the middle of Africa and you had never seen a stopwatch or known racing quite that way. If somebody told you that you are the world's fastest person and you could achieve something, it would give you a different perspective on your talent and how to use it. So my advice is if you learn early your talents, abilities, and personality, that knowledge can contribute to your success.

2. *Know Your Philosophy.* I also recommend that you know your mission and goals for your practice; what you stand for and what type of organization you are willing to work with.

3. *Know How You Define Success But Be Open to New Opportunities.* In each part of my career, I have looked at several issues to see how I defined success, and whether I had achieved it. It is critical to know what you want in your career; and what would make you happy and satisfied, whether it is money, control, independence, relationships, etc.

4. *Love Your Work.* Find a way in life to enjoy what you are doing. It is just not worth it unless you are having fun. But it doesn't mean that every moment is like being in Disney World. Remember, even at Disney World, sometimes you are in line. But choose something you love to do that you are passionate about. It is smart to really learn that about yourself, and have the luxury of working in a field you love. I feel sorry for people who hate what they do, but who have to make a living and have to do it. And fortunately, I have figured out how to make a living loving what I do. If I hadn't, I suspect that I would be much less happy.

5. *Find a Market Niche, But Don't Be Married to Your Niche.* You should find a niche but be open for the changes that will happen over a thirty- or forty-year period in your career. Something that is very important today in your field will absolutely be an afterthought twenty years from now. If you remain married to a narrow expertise, you will end up being the expert in something that nobody cares about. That is what happens to many academics. At twenty-seven, they decide to be an

expert in something, and forty years later they are the only person who still cares about their area of expertise.

6. *Embrace Change.* Challenge yourself to change, and if you don't like change, you better try to figure out how to deal with it or otherwise you are just going to see your career diminishing around you. Most people hate change, but if you can bring yourself to embrace it, you will be well positioned in the future. I find it very frustrating that people that I deal with don't like change. On the other hand, if everyone liked change as much as I did, I would be a lot less valuable. If you are open to change, you will have many career opportunities as I have had. For example, when I started speaking, I didn't do it for money, but one thing led to another, and it turned out to be a very complimentary line of business for me. So you may think that you were doing something for one purpose and maybe it did serve that purpose, but it also ended up serving many other purposes as well.

7. *Value Honesty, Integrity, and Professionalism.* People value someone who has integrity, so be up-front in addressing ethical issues with people. At the end of the day, all we ever have is our reputation. So value it. Understand it takes a long time to build and it can be destroyed very cheaply. Being a professional means taking seriously what you are doing, understanding that what happens to other people depends on what you do. Therefore, you better do the right thing. You better do at least what is ex-

pected of you, but try to do even more than what is expected of you. You must live up to your responsibilities; The Rockefeller Center situation is the perfect example of how I completed the job even though it took me many hours more than I had figured on. People pay you to be a professional. And we all get upset about an actor in a play or a ballplayer who is doing drugs or drinking because we feel that they are not able to give their best performance under those conditions. And by the way, physically, mentally, and emotionally, you should be as committed to your professional achievement as you want your favorite actor, singer, or ballplayer to be. Provide excellence in whatever you do and manage your time in order to complete your work on time. The real challenge is organizing your life in such a way that you can keep your productivity at a high level.

8. *Continue to Learn.* It is imperative you continue to learn in a variety of ways. It is just too competitive out there. If you are not learning and are bored, you will not be competitive. If you are open to new stimuli, then you are not driving the same road to work every day. And if you go back to my view that life is a journey, if all you do is drive the same road every day, it is going to get boring. I suggest you continue to learn through a wide range of sources as I do:

   - *Learn By Talking With People in a Variety of Circles.* Nobody has got the answer in business, so you must talk with all types of people in all types of fields. You find out the answer from little bits and snippets that are happening in the economy. For example, when I talk to people in business, I always ask them, 'So how's business?' And it's not an idle question. I am actually trying to get a little snippet of non-statistical information and figure out whether it is consistent with the data or not. Alan Greenspan is a master at that. Young people have different views. Older people have different views. So do people from the east, the west, and the south, people from different industries. One of the things, I think, that happens too often to people in academia, and sometimes in business, is people often talk to the same circle of people in their field all the time, but then you just hear your own opinions, your own ideas, your own value systems repeated. So try to talk with people in different fields.

- *Be Open to Learning New Technologies.* Always be open to learning new things like new technologies that are helpful and that make you more efficient. Technology will not replace relationships, but it will help you.

- *Read in a Wide Range of Fields.* I believe to keep up with current information, you must read in many different areas. I read a lot about real estate, but I also like reading new things, such as J.K. Rowling's work; I study German by reading novels in German.

- *Learn to See the 'Big Picture.'* It is very important to see the big picture in a situation, like in a Seurat painting. This is a hard skill for many to learn, because most business people, most students, most academics, are fixated on the color of a single dot. And the dot is good; somebody's got to put the dots there. But I think, especially if you're going to go into the advisory business, if you are going to go into the strategic part of business like running a company, you have got to be able to step back from the dots and see the pattern, see the picture. The dot is good, but it is the picture that matters. So train yourself to see the big picture in a situation.

- *Learn from Receiving a Formal Education:*

A. *A Formal Education Helps You Gain Analytical and Research Skills.* You learn the skill by making a mistake and you are not punished for mistakes. If you think about what education is about, it is very much more about making mistakes than getting things right. It is a controlled environment where being wrong is not so severely punished. If in three months you can make a year's worth of mistakes, that is very beneficial. If you were wrong in real life as often as you are wrong in a classroom or in writing a term paper, you would get fired. I get frustrated sometimes with students who focus on grades instead of getting information to add to their repertoire and move forward. Think about why you go to a batting cage before you hit. You go because you learn how to miss the ball a lot on your own. So in academia you are in a setting where you learn how to do things better and you are not punished for making mistakes. It is like going to a batting cage.

B. *Education Gives You Credentials.* If there are no good programs in your field, you are not at a disadvantage in not having a formal education. In my generation there were no good real estate programs, so you took an economics degree, or a finance degree, an urban design degree, or maybe a law degree when there were no real estate degrees available. Today, there are a lot of good real estate programs, so you are at a disadvantage without that education and it shows in the job market. Does that mean you will not succeed? Of course not. People succeed in all sorts of strange and wondrous ways. But taking advantage of a formal education in your field allows you to learn the skills set, the knowledge set, and get great contacts. Better programs like the Wharton Center bring in great people, brighter students, and create excitement.

9. *Build Relationships*: All types of relationships are key to success:

- *Build a Network.* Success in any business comes through word of mouth, recommendations, and referrals. You must have the ability to get and keep clients, and build relationships.

- *Value Mentors in Your Life.* I believe at the end of my career, it is the relationships that I have built that will be important in how I view my success and satisfaction in my career. Lucille Ford turned me on to economics and teaching, and helped me understand my talents. She pointed out that I had an unusual set of gifts, and advised me on how to use them. We have built a wonderful friendship. Marshall Bennett has also been a tremendous support to me, and from that friendship we have worked on several projects, like creating the Real Estate School at Roosevelt University in Chicago.

- *Mentor Others.* When you help others with their careers, you gain as much as you give. If you are a reasonably good teacher, that is, I believe, a real responsibility in life. I am not a religious person. If you don't want my advice, I am not going to force it on you. But if you seek it, I have a responsibility to tell you what and why I think it and try to help you understand it. And if it does not connect, then it doesn't connect.

"By the way, sometimes you are the mentee, and sometimes you are the mentor, but the relationships are always valuable. I think when I look back, at the end of my life on my deathbed, I have a suspicion that I will remember the students, faculty, people that I mentored or who have mentored me as a big part of what my success and my happiness were about. In a long career, when you look back, the relationships you make are key to your happiness.

Someone like Lucille Ford or Marshall Bennett in your life can help you learn and move forward in your career.

10. *Understand People Are People.* As I told you in the chapter for ASTD, when I think back over the past thirty years that I have been teaching, practicing and consulting, I see that people still have the same concerns. They still want to make money and live well. Yes, the tax laws are very different, the oil prices are different, the enemies are very different, but people are the same, and they want the same general things in life. It is important in your career to know the factors that will change from the ones that will remain the same, because it will greatly impact your career.

11. *Develop Good Communication Skills.* Communication skills, especially listening skills, are essential in every field. Writing, speaking, and being a moderator are all great ways to develop ways to communicate with your audience.

12. *Be a Good Team Player.* I learned the skills for working well in teams in college when I played football, and now I play basketball. In academic life, as in many other fields, you often work alone, but you still have times when you must be able to work productively as part of a team. If you learn the skills for working well in teams, you will be able to build better relationship with your clients, colleagues, and people in organizations.

13. *Learn How to Deal With Challenges and Move On.* Learn to move

forward regardless of events. Everybody's had a friend who died, illnesses in their family, and challenges at work. Some people cope with them and prosper and take on new relationships as a result of it, and others break down. Everybody runs into rough patches. The question is not, *Do you have rough patches?* The question is, *How do you survive your rough patches?* How do you find other alternatives? And so, my answer is you just do the best that you are capable of doing. I know it is very philosophical, but I believe that you must move forward to enjoy your life regardless of challenges and obstacles.

14. *Stay Healthy By Having Balance in Your Life.* Assemble your priorities. My father died right after my freshman year in college, and I was struck by the fact that the world just went right on. And I understand the world is going to go right on after me. So I take everything I do seriously, but I try not to take myself too seriously! I try to work out and create a balanced life. Part of maintaining health is to exercise regularly. A healthy body allows for a healthy mind. Staying in shape is essential to have the ability to do the job, especially as one gets older. To be alert and do the job, you need to stay in shape. Working out not only helps you think, but is also enjoyable. You can always find an extra half hour."

Advice on Success from Peter

Q: What is the best advice you could give somebody for career success?

LINNEMAN: "I would say four things to you: First, find something that you love to do. If you want to succeed, it is just too hard to beat other people if you dislike what you're doing. It doesn't matter whether or not they're as smart as you. They have the same hours in a day, and they have the same drive. The only advantage you have got is to find something that turns you on. And I find that constantly getting new stimuli, different stimuli, changing what I look at and how I look at it, is what keeps me turned on.

"Second, do not try to always think about what you will get out of doing something, because if you do, you will probably get nothing most of the time. You should view it as 'this is just what the journey is.' You take in the sights as you are going down the road.

"Third, a student once asked me, 'How do I get a Rolodex® like yours?' And I said, 'It's very easy. Do right by people as best you can for thirty years and do not hurt anybody intentionally, and I promise you, you will have a good Rolodex®.'

"Last, and most important, I still would advise you as I did in the interview for a chapter in ASTD (2002), 'Building a World-Renowned Practice: Linneman Associates,' that having a successful career should be a 'Journey—not a destination.' You should know where the stops are, know where your challenges and your obstacles are, but most importantly, enjoy the journey.

"Several years ago, I was with Samuel Zell, chairman of several U.S. and international corporations, when a student came up to him on campus and said, 'I want to be just like you in five years.' To which he responded, 'Why do you think it will take you only five years, when it took me forty?'

"Sam is so bright that those words really hit me; and students are sick of me telling this story, but he is 100 percent correct. A good career should be a journey, not a destination. I mentor many students on how to achieve success in their careers. Students always want their success to happen overnight. But building a career is more about the journey and building relationships than overnight success. When you run too fast in basketball, you trip over your own feet. You need to run fast, but you do not need to run so fast that you trip over your own feet. When you are young and bright and energetic, you are excited about being successful. Sometimes you have to step back and let the game come to you. Patience is a virtue. Know where the stops are in your career, but enjoy the journey."

Author's Concluding Tips

Dr. Peter Linneman's story is powerful because he has had career success in many different fields simultaneously, and because of it, he has been able to reach a level of success that many people only dream about. But he has been up-front and honest about giving you the insight into how he has done so. And perhaps, as he did, you can build a career doing several things to reach your peak and fulfill all your career needs. For example, you could be a social worker, love the work, but not make enough money in that job to live the lifestyle you desire, so you develop other talents in your field by writing, speaking, and consulting to add to your career. Use the insight from these stories to find your perfect career path; it will lead you to a lifetime of career opportunities that is right for you. I will end with what I believe are the most valuable lessons that I have learned from these stories that can guide you to your perfect career. I call it *My Prescription for Success*, after Oprah's "What I Know for Sure." This is mine:

What I Know for Sure:

➤ *Use the 7 Steps in this Book.* It will move you forward in your path for success.

➤ *Learn a Field You Love that Matches Your Unique Talents.* If you love your work, it will set you on your path. If you are not passionate about your work, it is too competitive to succeed.

➤ *Find Your Niche and Try to Be the Best At It.* Know what your competitors are doing, but do not focus on them. It will take energy away from your ability to use your unique talents to find what is perfect for you.

➤ *Learn Your Failings, But Play to Your Strengths.* Try to avoid positions that do not play to your strengths.

➤ *Work Hard in Whatever You Do.* It will lead you forward to new opportunities that you are unaware of until they happen.

➤ *Build a Plan.* With a plan, you have something to follow every day.

➤ *Be Open to Changes.* Make sure your talents are aligned with what is happening in your context and in the world. For example, Patricia Choi said if you are in the right place at the right time, your skills will lead to success. And as Peter Linneman points out, you must be open to changes that occur and adapt in your career.

➤ *Build Relationships.* Through being a mentor or mentee, and teaching, you will get back more than you give, and nobody truly succeeds on his or her own.

➤ *Stay Healthy.* Always take time to exercise and eat right; you can be much more successful if you have the energy and health for your field.

➤ *Continue to Learn.* All types of education can help you advance in your career. Learn by reading, talking, acquiring both a formal and informal education and training in your field through workshops, degrees, licenses, designations, continuing education courses, and etc.

➤ *Have Fun Regardless.* In all good things there are difficult tasks.

➤ *Build Career Sidelines.* You can use your talents to combine several career fields into one by consulting, speaking, teaching, writing, etc., and have a much more successful career, both financially and personally.

➤ *Value Your Reputation.* Think of what happens to famous people in the news when they are involved in a scandal—most business people do not want to be associated with you.

➤ *Turn Negatives Into Positives.* As the saying goes, "If you have lemons, make lemonade."

➤ *Learn How You Deal with Challenges and Obstacles.* Everyone has a pattern. Learn what yours is and use it to move forward.

➤ *Challenge Yourself to Go for What You Want.*

➤ *Do Not Let Fear Stop You.* I believe what Susan Jeffers says: "Feel the fear and do it anyway."

➤ *Take Time to Reflect.* Every week, take time to reflect on your career, and at least once a year, reflect on your career and your life, and celebrate your accomplishments.

➤ *Learn What You Stand For.* Learn what you believe in, what your values are, and how you define success. The earlier in life, the better.

In the end, I could not have given you a better philosophy to guide you than **Peter Linneman's** words:

"Know where the stops are,
where the challenges are,
but enjoy the journey."

Suggested Reading

Apps, Jerold W. *Study Skills for Adults Returning to School*, and other books on www.Amazon.com.

Bolles, Richard-Nelson. (2004). *What Color is Your Parachute? A Practical Manual for Job Hunters and Career-changers.* Berkeley, CA: Ten Speed Press.

Brem, Caroline. *Returning to Learning: Studying as an Adult: Tips, Traps and Triumphs.* www.Amazon.com.

Combs, Patrick. (2003). *Major in Success: Make College Easier, Fire Up Your Dreams, and Get a Very Cool Job.* Berkeley, CA: Ten Speed Press.

Jeffers, Susan. *Feel the Fear and Do It Anyway.* Books and tapes on www.Amazon.com.

Suggested References

Dictionary of Occupational Titles. Fourth Edition Revised. Bureau of Labor Statistics Washington, D.C.: U.S. Department of Labor.

National Trade and Professional Association of the United States NTPA (updated annually). Look up any professional associations.

Occupational Outlook Handbook. (2004-2005). U.S. Department of Labor, Bureau of Labor Statistics. Washington, D.C.: U.S. Government Printing Office or www.Amazon.com.

Suggested Job Employment Web Sites

1. Best Jobs USA
www.bestjobsusa.com
2. Career Builder
www.careerbuilder.com

3. Career Magazine
www.careermag.com

4. Chicago Tribune
www.chicagotribune.com

5. College Grad Job Hunter
www.collegegrad.com

6. CollegeRecruiter.com
www.collegerecruiter.com

7. Crain's Chicago Business Online
www.crainschicagobusiness.com

8. FlipDog.com
www.flipdog.com

9. Hoovers Online
www.hoovers.com

10. Hot Jobs
www.hotjobs.com

11. Job Bank USA
www.jobbankusa.com

12. Job Web.org
www.jobweb.org

13. Jobs Online
www.jobsonline.com

14. Monster.com
www.monster.com

15. Retired Brains
www.retiredbrains.com

16. Salary.com
www.salary.com

17. 6 Figure Jobs.com
www.6figurejobs.com

18. True Careers
www.jobdirect.com

19. Virtual Job Fair
www.brassring.com

20. Wet Feet
www.wetfeet.com

About the Author

Why I teach others how to find their perfect careers?

Dr. Margot B. Weinstein is an internationally well-known practitioner, educator, writer, consultant, and speaker in business and education with over thirty years' experience. Dr. Weinstein is vice president of Kingston Group Inc. and president and CEO of MW Leadership Consultants LLC.

When she graduated high school, her dream was to be a college professor. With her grades, abilities, and college entrance test scores, her high school counselors suggested that she attend a top university in the United States. However, her parents did not approve. Her parents were foreign born: Her father was from Poland, and her mother was from Russia, and they did not believe that a woman needed a college degree. Furthermore, they wanted her to work in the field of business instead of education. So, they requested that she attend only one year of college full-time under very strict guidelines and then find a job in business. At the time, children usually honored their parents' requests.

Although Dr. Weinstein always found something she loved and has been very successful in each of her two career fields, as a leader in the clothing industry and as a co-owner of a commercial real estate company, she continued to dream of receiving a college degree so she could teach and mentor others. Over the years, she attended seven universities and community colleges at night, including Northwestern. At that time, you could not complete a B.A. degree part-time at night school. Although several colleges had offered her full scholarships to attend their programs, because of financial and family responsibilities, she continued to put her dreams on hold.

In 1990, she returned to college (after raising four children with her husband) so that she could finally teach other returning adult students. Within seven and a half years, she received four college degrees with honors while continuing to work. Dr. Weinstein received a B.A. in 1992, two master's degrees—one in adult education in 1994 and one in psychology in 1997, and her doctoral degree in 1998. Also, she completed post-doctoral credits in Russia and Finland in 2000, and she earned her International Real Estate Specialist Designation (CIPS) from the National Association of REALTORS® in 2002.

Even though Dr. Weinstein never changed her goals and her dreams of returning to college to learn to design programs for adults, when she was completing her post-doctoral work in Russia in 2000 with Professors John Niemi and Gene Roth, she finally began to understand her parents' values toward women in education and business.

So that she could succeed as a returning adult student, parent, and businesswoman, she designed this "7 Step Process," and later discovered that her process and strategies fit the stories of successful people she had interviewed on their careers. In the past several years, she has interviewed two hundred people (one hundred leaders) of major organizations worldwide on their careers, such as Sam Zell, Chairman, Equity Group Investments LLC; Eugene Golub, Chairman, Golub & Company; and John Baird, Chairman, Baird & Warner. She has written and speaks about her career process, strategies, and insights from her interviews to adults in organizations, universities, and colleges worldwide.

Dr. Weinstein believes passionately that everyone has a unique talent, and you should find it and utilize it to create your perfect career journey—and the earlier in life, the better. So she wrote this book in the hopes that it can help you achieve your perfect career.

More Ways to Learn to Achieve Career Success

Regardless of what field you want to become successful in,
Dr. Margot B. Weinstein will show you how. Dr. Weinstein teaches
strategies she has learned from interviewing very successful people
throughout the world for the past ten years on how they have
achieved success. Dr. Weinstein will teach you how to achieve
success and make your dream a reality.

Bring Dr. Weinstein to your next convention or meeting and transform your group and learn strategies for unbelievable success.

- **Book** her for a Speaking Event or Workshop
- **Sign up** for her Workshops & Seminars
- **Order** her Publications or Audio Tapes

Dr. Margot B. Weinstein
President & CEO, MW Leadership Consultants LLC
Vice President, Kingston Group Inc.
1040 N. Lake Shore Drive, 34C
Chicago, IL 60611
312-664-4849; FAX: 312-664-4869
Email: drmargot@drmargotweinstein.com
www.drmargotweinstein.com

To order additional copies of *7 Steps to Find Your Perfect Career*
(ISBN-10: 0-9760732-0-X; ISBN-13: 978-0-9760732-0-X)
($14.95 each—$20.00 includes shipping/handling), or to inquire
about multiple or bulk copies, please contact Dr. Weinstein directly.